ISAIAH'S
OPEN BOOK

ISAIAH'S
OPEN BOOK

A book for the Church

MICHAEL E. W. THOMPSON

CHURCH IN THE MARKET PLACE
PUBLICATIONS • *WARRINGTON*
2008

British Library Cataloguing in Publication Data

A record for this book is available from the British Library

ISBN 978-1-899147-66-3

CHURCH IN THE MARKET PLACE PUBLICATIONS

Typeset in Monotype Baskerville by
Patricia Saunders, Huntingdon

Printed in Great Britain by
Ralph Wrightsons Ltd, Earls Barton

CONTENTS

PREFACE

What follows is offered to the interested general reader as an introduction to the book of Isaiah. For the title of the work, *Isaiah's Open Book*, I am indebted to that of a book published over a decade ago, *The Open Text: New Directions for Biblical Studies?* The editor of that volume, Francis Watson, acknowledged that the language about the 'open text' comes from Martin Luther, in particular from his Preface to his early lectures on the Psalms where he speaks of his concern about such biblical texts: 'lest we become burdened with a closed book and receive no food'.[1]

My concern is that in the Church today in this part of the world the book of Isaiah (along with very much else in the Old Testament) remains largely a 'closed book', and in what follows I make my own modest attempt to 'open' it so as to help others 'open' this particular part of the Bible for themselves, and thus find 'food' within it both for their own lives and maybe also for their groups and even congregations. Hence my subtitle, *A book for the Church*, which I intend, somewhat immodestly, to carry a double meaning. In the first place I wish to help us in the Church to open the book of Isaiah and to find food to sustain us in our worship, witness and service, in short to find that the book of Isaiah can be an 'open book' for us today in the Church. In the second place I offer what follows here as a little book 'for the Church'; there is I fear nothing here for the Academy, though it is from there that I have learned so much about the Isaiah book. I seek here to pass on something of that for the benefit and – thinking of Luther's concern that we receive no food – some sustenance for the Church.

I go about this project in two main ways, represented by the two parts of the work, these being separated by the 'Intermezzo: The book completed and ready to be opened'. Following on from

an introductory Prelude, in Part One I simply work through the
Isaiah book, trying to help whoever will read it to see 'the wood
for the trees' in this very large biblical book. I seek to show what
are the different parts and sections of the book, and how they join
together so that the whole does have a real, satisfying, and logical
structure. I discuss issues of authorship of the parts of the book,
and something of what apparently must have been editorial
processes that resulted in the book of Isaiah we have in our Bibles.

In Part Two I offer three pieces, all of which have been presented at various times to church groups, largely to preachers and
leaders of worship, but by no means exclusively. In the Postlude I
offer a sermon, and this on the basis that if Isaiah is to be a true
part of the 'open book' of the Bible for the Church then there
must surely be material here for the Church's proclamation today.
In Part Two, and in that Postlude, I do not in any way claim to
have reached any very satisfactory goals in opening up the Isaiah
book, but I would like to think that my efforts might encourage
others to make their own attempts, and hopefully do better where
I have fallen short. Further, in this part of the work I am aware of
a certain amount of repetition, but have felt on balance that each
of the pieces should be left essentially as it was when originally
delivered. I am also aware that I do not have any discussion here
about the place of the Old Testament in the life of the Church
today, and in particular concerning those processes by which we
take a document from long ago and 'apply' it to our lives today in
our very different situations from those of the author(s) and editors of that work. This is a subject to which I hope I may return
elsewhere.

There are two books with which I am in a certain amount of
conversation in this work, and with which I see it as having some
sort of family relationship, in particular having sought to keep in
mind and and to write for the same general readership. These are
the volumes of the Epworth Commentary series on the book of
Isaiah, that on chapters 1 to 39 by David Stacey, and that on
chapters 40 to 66 by myself, following David Stacey's sad death.
It is these commentaries to which in general terms I make first

reference for 'further details' on this passage, or that issue, and in each case I cite them briefly in the form, Stacey, *Isaiah 1–39*, Thompson, *Isaiah 40–66*, with the appropriate page numbers. There are also a number of other commentaries on Isaiah that I cite in this short-title form, and full details of all of these, and of various other works which I think may be of help and interest to readers of this present volume, will be found in the Select Bibliography. My biblical quotations are from NRSV.

I do thank all those without whose contributions this little work would not be seeing the light of day. I think of many colleagues and friends in the Church with whom I have worked over the years and who have borne patiently yet encouragingly with what must have appeared to be my growing preoccupation with the book of Isaiah, to those groups who have invited me to speak to them on this part of the Bible, to an annual conference of the Methodist Sacramental Fellowship that made me so very welcome and then with commendable fortitude heard three lectures on Isaiah, even publishing them in their 1999 Bulletin. I am now most grateful to the Revd Robert Davies and Church in the Market Place Publications for bringing this work into print. Once again, and in a league all on her own, there has been the loving presence and help of my wife, Hazel. At a practical level in certain moments of crisis her computing skills – which far, far exceed mine – were called upon, and never did my cry go unheard.

MICHAEL E. W. THOMPSON
Farnsfield, Nottinghamshire
Feast of St John Chrysostom,
Preacher, Bishop of Constantinople
13 September 2007

ABBREVIATIONS

AD	Anno Domini
BC	Before Christ
BCE	Before the Common Era
CE	The Common Era
ed.	editor/edited
ExpTim	*Expository Times*
Int	*Interpretation*
JSOT	*Journal for the Study of the Old Testament*
JSOTSup	*Journal for the Study of the Old Testament* Supplement Series
NRSV	New Revised Standard Version of the Bible, 1989
REB	Revised English Bible, 1989
tr.	Translator
ZAW	*Zeitschrift für die alttestamentliche Wissenschaft*
1QIs^a	First Isaiah Scroll from Qumran
1QIs^b	Second Isaiah Scroll from Qumran

PRELUDE

By way of introduction

What Christians are accustomed to call the eighth century BC [1] was an age of stirring new works and deeds, and not in one country alone. For in the land that we call Greece a remarkable poet named Homeros, usually known to us as Homer, was active and would produce his remarkable epic poems, the *Iliad* and the *Odyssey*. Then also, in Assyria was the coming to power, to leadership not only in the national but also in the international sphere, of Tiglath-pileser III, a remarkable military man whose presence would have such an effect upon many of the states of the Ancient Near East, for he would extend his nation's lands and seek to secure its borders in the West. [2]

Meanwhile in the, comparatively tiny, country of Judah, with its capital city of Jerusalem, there was the prophet Isaiah, son of a certain Amoz (about whom, apart from his name, we know nothing), whose theological interpretation of history would be on a much grander scale, altogether of a new order, from anything that others of his people had previously fashioned and were fashioning. Further, this attempt at interpreting what was going on around them in the light of their faith in, and their belief in the lordship of their God, Yahweh, would have a remarkable potentiality to generate further theological interpretations of history. These further and new theological interpretations were needed because those changes that the Assyrian ruler Tiglath-pileser III brought about for the people of Judah and Jerusalem – and also those for the peoples of the neighbouring countries – were by no means the last changes that they would experience. Far from it, for rather they would come to find themselves being caught up in and involved in a long and ongoing series of changes in their

I

wider political, military, cultural, and even religious situations and surroundings. For the fact was that mighty in its day though it was, the Assyrian empire would not last for ever, and would fall eventually to Babylonian power, and that in its turn to Persian. All this is to say that the historical situation for these people kept changing as their ongoing march of life continued, and that these circumstances kept calling forth the 'word of the Lord' for each new situation, each new age; a new word, even new words, for each of the new epochs.

Our subject is the book of Isaiah, one of the longest books in the Hebrew Bible, what Christians call the Old Testament. But as well as being a long book, it is also one – as we shall come to see in what follows – that displays a range of styles, and whose contents are very varied. As well as having thrilling messages of hope for the future, there are also doom-laden passages expressing the most severe judgement upon God's people; alongside some of the Old Testament's most sublime poetical passages there are stories recorded in prose that read much like a part of the books of Kings; here are warnings of a coming exile, yet here also is thrilling news that exile is coming to an end and that people can return home to Jerusalem; here are passages detailing the failings of kings, yet also the vision of a king, or kings, who will rule in wisdom and righteousness. And here also are passages about a servant – and servants. So much, in short, within the compass of one book, or – perhaps we should say – within one scroll, for it would have been on a scroll that the book of Isaiah was first written. [3]

The book of Isaiah opens with a title, which speaks of the word God gave to his prophet Isaiah, and of the time when this took place, during the reigns of which kings. Thus,

> The vision of Isaiah, son of Amoz, which he saw concerning Judah and Jerusalem in the days of Uzziah, Jotham, Ahaz, and Hezekiah, kings of Judah. (Isaiah 1.1)

Now we know of these kings from the books of Kings, and also in that alternative presentation of Judean history in the books of Chronicles, and though precision in these matters is not possible, it is likely that Uzziah reigned in Jerusalem 783–742 BC, Jotham 742–735, Ahaz 735–715, and Hezekiah 715–687.[4] Yet with the last-named of these kings we are still a long way from the people of Judah and Jerusalem going into exile in Babylon (587 BC), and even further from their coming out of exile and returning to their homeland and capital city, that is sometime after Cyrus the Persian made his triumphal entry into Babylon, bringing to an end the Babylonian empire, in 539 BC. That is, what are we to understand about the authorship of the parts of the book of Isaiah that speak of times *after* the reign of Hezekiah? Who was responsible for them? Certainly, the prophet Isaiah cannot have been present, alive in 539 BC, that is some two hundred years later! Some people argue that the prophet Isaiah saw all these things in vision, that all this was given to him in vision, or by some other means, by the Lord. But if that is so, then why is it that that is not stated in the title of the book? Why does the list of kings in Isaiah 1.1 conclude with Hezekiah? Much more likely, it seems to many of us, that what we have in the book of Isaiah is not only the prophecies of Isaiah the son of Amoz, but also those of other prophets as well, and moreover the contributions of editors – or as they are more usually known in biblical studies, redactors.[5]

One place in the book of Isaiah where it is particularly clear that there is a change of style and background is at the beginning of chapter 40. In an immediate and dramatic way we are confronted here with words of hope, reassurance, all concerned it seems, with the glowing and exciting possibilities of a new start for the people of Israel.[6] Further, this theme continues in the chapters that follow, with the result that the material in these chapters is markedly different from what has gone before. It is not that there is no note of hope in what has preceded. Far from it. Yet what is different in Isaiah 40 and what follows is that we are not reading isolated passages that speak in hopeful tones, but rather a whole series of chapters that joys in, and overflows with assurances of hope and new possibilities for the people of Israel. The most likely setting for this material would seem to be the closing years of Israel's exile in Babylon, in particular the time of the

arrival in military and political triumph of Cyrus the Persian
ruler who would proclaim to his subject people that they were
henceforth free both to worship their own gods and also to return
to their own lands.

Thus it is, as we shall see in what follows, that scholars have
isolated chapters 40 to 55 as apparently having come from an historical background different from, later than that of the ministry
of the prophet Isaiah of Jerusalem spoken about in the very first
verse of the book that bears his name. Further, and also as we
shall come to see below, it appears that with Isaiah 56 and the following chapters we have further new material, material now that
appears to have come from an even later time, from a time when
apparently the people of Israel are back in Jerusalem seeking to
rebuild the city, the temple, individual lives, communal and religious life. The most likely setting for this material would seem to
be the period after the return from exile, made possible by the
decrees of the Persian ruler Cyrus.

Yet we should not go away with the impression that these
blocks of material have simply been put together for random, ad
hoc reasons, as if, say, together they made up a convenient
amount of writings to go onto one scroll. Rather, and once again
we shall observe the details of this in what follows, there are evidences to suggest that all the various parts of the book have been
purposefully put together, and further, that all the parts are
intended to be read as part of, making up, one whole piece of
writing. We are given two particular clues that lead us to this conclusion, the first being in the occurrence of certain words and
various expressions that occur throughout the different parts of
the book, some of them not occurring very frequently in the Old
Testament outside the book of Isaiah. An example of this is the
expression used of God, the 'Holy One of Israel'. This occurs a
significant number of times throughout the book of Isaiah, but
not very often outside it. Then there is surely something significant about the whole shape of the work. While from a historical
point of view the book of Isaiah takes us through various aspects
of the life of the people of Judah and Jerusalem – at first as they

enjoyed political independence, being ruled by their own kings, and then later under the successive rules of the Assyrians, the Babylonians, and the Persians – when looked at from a thematic and theological point of view we can see how it speaks of judgement, forgiveness, and restoration.

In order to explain how we have come to have this completed book of Isaiah before us we should perhaps imagine a follower, or a number of followers, of the prophet Isaiah who prophesied in the city of Jerusalem in the eighth century BC, and who sought to record his words, his speeches, his warnings to his people, along with the expressions of hope and reassurance for them in the future which he believed had been given to him by the Lord. But then imagine time going by and the realisation coming to this follower, these followers of the prophet that things in the world were changing and that surely what Isaiah had said in the past now needed some 'updating' to make it appropriate for the new situation. Further, imagine that perhaps others came to feel that they too had been called by God to be prophets and to speak the divine word to a new situation, yet feeling themselves to be people who understood things rather in the way that Isaiah the son of Amoz had done, who perhaps regarded themselves as 'disciples' (see Isaiah 8.16) of the master. While they may, as we might express it, have taken the same sort of line as he did, thought in the same way as he did, had a similar approach to such things, yet they saw that the times were changing, and that if Isaiah were now in his prime and prophesying *now* then perhaps he would be saying rather different things. And imagine too that sooner or later, and most likely later, the need of the contribution of an editor, or a number of editors, who would bring the whole work to completion in that form we know, the form of the book of Isaiah that has come down to us.

Now the end point of that whole process we can to some extent pinpoint historically, because a scroll of the completed book of Isaiah was found among the Qumran scrolls, more commonly called the Dead Sea Scrolls. Further, the writer of the book of Ecclesiasticus, Ben Sirach when he speaks of Isaiah is clearly speaking of the book that we know. We shall return to this matter, but for the present it is sufficient to say that the upshot of it is that by about 100 BC the book of Isaiah as we have it had been completed.[7] Clearly much theological and literary work had gone into the making of the completed whole, and henceforth it would be the subject of close study by both Jewish and Christian scholars. Perhaps more importantly – and no doubt more in tune with the purposes for which it had over long centuries been written and edited by a considerable number of people, and thus eventually completed – its words were read, not only in private but also in corporate worship, again by both Jews and Christians.

In this brief prelude to this work large claims have been made for the book of Isaiah, that it deals with a series of large themes, that it sets out so much of the life of the people of God through a series of worldly changes, that it seeks to interpret those events and that people's history in terms of God's purposes for them and for others. Justification for and the necessary explanation of such claims will, I hope, be found in what follows in the remainder of this work. But for the present that is enough by way of introduction: the time has come to consider the contents of the book, and this we do in Part One of this work, which now follows. So we go to 'The Book of Isaiah'.

PART ONE

THE BOOK OF ISAIAH

I

CHAPTERS I TO 39

Here in chapters 1 to 39 is the first main block of material into which the book of Isaiah falls, the others being chapters 40 to 55 and 56 to 66. As we shall see, there is a wide variety of material in chapters 1 to 39, some of which appears to come from the eighth century BC, and could well come from the prophet Isaiah of Jerusalem. Yet there are other parts of these chapters that for a variety of reasons look as if they must come from rather later times and therefore possibly not from Isaiah. Frequently, what appears to be the historical background to such passages does not look like an eighth-century setting. Sometimes these matters will be considered as we come to the passages in question, but at other times because it is difficult to be sure about the background situation and thus about the date we shall leave the matter open. Whatever may have been the time from which a particular passage came, and whether it came from Isaiah, or whether from another prophet, or whether from an editor, this we do know – that at some stage or other it came to be incorporated into the book of Isaiah.

Chapter 1: God's complaint
It was good number of years ago that the suggestion was made that this chapter was intended to be an introduction to what follows, and this is now widely accepted. [1] It is akin to an overture to a musical work, a recital of some of the main themes that will make themselves heard in the main body of the composition. Thus it is that after the introductory verse in 1.1 has provided the title to the book, and given details of the historical period in which the prophet Isaiah was commissioned by the Lord to speak

9

in his name to the people of Judah and Israel, that in 1.2–3 we
are introduced to the first of these themes. This is one of the fundamental themes of the whole of the book of Isaiah, one which,
as we shall see, makes its presence felt right up to the last chapter.
It is the theme of the sin of God's people, and in graphic and
memorable language and imagery it is presented to us:

> Hear, O heavens, and listen, O earth;
>   for the Lord has spoken:
> I reared children and brought them up,
>   but they have rebelled against me.
> The ox knows its owner,
>   and the donkey its master's crib;
> but Israel does not know,
>   my people do not understand. (Isaiah 1.2–3)

The speaker here is the Lord, and he is making his complaint
about the conduct of his people. We are invited in this imagery
to picture him taking his people to court, and as befits a plaintiff
of such exalted status as the Lord God, nothing less than the
heavens and the earth are called to be his witnesses, witnesses to
the fact that his people have forsaken and betrayed him in a quite
breathtaking fashion. Moreover, they have behaved totally without sense. Why, even the animals behave with more sense! The ox
and the donkey show more appreciation of their dependence
upon their master than do the people of Israel upon their God!
This 'trial scene' imagery, as it is called, will recur in the book of
Isaiah, becoming particularly prominent in chapters 40 to 55.[2]

We need at this point to take note of the name 'Israel' in verse
3. Right at the beginning of the book, in 1.1, we read about the
vision that Isaiah had concerning 'Judah and Jerusalem'. The
main focus of the prophecies of Isaiah does seem to have been
the southern kingdom of Judah, with its capital city Jerusalem.
There are perhaps some places where in chapters 1 to 39 oracles
are addressed to the northern kingdom of Israel, that being
addressed as 'Israel' or 'Ephraim' (as in 9.8–9, 12, 14). That
(northern) kingdom of Israel came to an end at the hands of the

Assyrian army in 722 BC. However at other times 'Israel' appears
to refer to the whole nation (as in 1.3; 8.14, 19, and as in the
divine title 'Holy One of Israel'). Later in the book, particularly
in chapters 40 to 55, 'Israel' will be used simply as the name of
the people of God.
Then, verses 4–9 speak about the parlous state into which
Israel has descended as a result of its people's sinful behaviour.
The fact is that they are grievous sinners (v. 4), and the whole
body of the nation has no soundness in it. It is a deep sickness
that is described in verses 5 and 6:

> The whole head is sick,
>   and the whole heart faint.
> From the sole of the foot even to the head,
>   there is no soundness in it,
> but bruises and sores
>   and bleeding wounds;
> they have not been drained, or bound up,
>   or softened with oil. (Isaiah 1.5–6)

Further, their countryside has taken on an abandoned and devastated appearance (v. 7), the cities being charred ruins, the countryside desolate, all alike occupied by foreign invaders. We will
return to the invaders spoken about here, but in the meantime we
need to take note of the reference in the following verse (v. 8) to
'daughter Zion'. This is Jerusalem, the principal city of Judah
that in the book of Isaiah is frequently called Zion, and at times,
as here, daughter of Zion (see also 3.16–17; 4.4; 10.32; 16.1;
37.22). In the book of Isaiah we also find such expressions in
regard to other cities, for example 'daughter of Tarshish' in 23.10
and 'daughter of Sidon' in 23.12. It has frequently been suggested
that the historical setting of the words of v. 8,

> And daughter Zion is left
>   like a booth in a vineyard,
> like a shelter in a cucumber field,
>   like a besieged city

is that of the dreadful siege of Jerusalem by the Assyrian ruler
Sennacherib in 701 BC when he conquered the surrounding
towns, villages and countryside, and when indeed Jerusalem on its
own was the only city able to withstand the enemy. Even so, it was
a 'besieged city'. [3] That may well have been the original setting of
these words, and yet it is important to take note of the fact that
they have been adapted so as to serve here in what appears to be
the introductory chapter to the whole book. They now serve to
give something of a warning to people of all ages, to those who
will read this book, to those who will hear its words, that the con-
sequencies of turning away from the pursuit of the way and the
will of God is dangerous indeed and beset with many perils. This
is a theme that we shall observe recurring as we read on in the
book of Isaiah.

In the following verses (vv. 10–17) we are introduced to another
topic of fundamental concern in the book of Isaiah. This is worship, and what is spoken about here is both its abuse and also its
correct observance. Verses 10–15 are about worship that is offered
to God, but by people whose lives are unworthy, unrighteous.
Here is God being worshipped and invoked by people who have
caused bloodshed (v. 15), and it is being stated in the strongest
terms that this is nothing less than an abomination to the Lord.
What, rather, God requires is worship that springs from lives in
which there is the daily pursuit of justice and righteousness. Thus
to these people, both sinful and deluded, comes the word of the
Lord through his prophet:

> Wash yourselves; make yourselves clean;
>> remove the evil of your doings
>> from before my eyes;
> cease to do evil
>> learn to do good;
> seek justice,
>> rescue the oppressed,
> defend the orphan,
>> plead for the widow. (Isaiah 1.16–17)

Then in verses 18–20 comes the divine appeal to these sinful people to amend their lives, to accept the offer of God's forgiveness. It is an appeal that people will be obedient to the will of God. By this means these people will be granted the opportunity to enjoy the fruits of the 'good life' that God offers to them. So we come to verses 21–26, a passage which speaks eloquently of the Lord's sadness over the city that once was faithful. No details are given about when this blissful state prevailed, but rather it is a generalised statement, the sort of statement that is made in age after age when thinking and concerned people perceive a decline in standards from those that have prevailed in earlier days and better times. The particular observation highlighted in these verses is that whereas in the past the city was full of justice – no doubt something of an exaggeration, but one that we easily recognise, and that we can accept as making the intended point – now it is full of assassins, and once again we spot the element of exaggeration as that point is made. [4] In fact, so many deplorable reverses in the life of the city have occurred, these being expressed in a series of images: what was silver has been turned to dross, wine has become watered down, princes have become rebels. There are yet more horrors to be catalogued: while there is a love of bribes and gifts, there is at the same time no care for the future of orphans or for the plight of widows. Upon such unmindful and neglectful people the Lord's judgement – so the prophet proclaims – must inevitably come. Yet here also is the promise that out of that searing time of judgement future good may come: one day there will once again be good judges and counsellors, there will be a rebirth of the city of righteousness, the faithful city.

It is time to pause and to take stock of what we have been thinking about in this opening chapter of the Isaiah book. Is it possible to say something about the background situation of what has been spoken about in these verses? To what extent and in what ways will these themes appear later in Isaiah? How may these words, these concerns, impact upon our lives, maybe to speak something of God's word to us today in our, inevitably, very different lives and world?

Some of the material in Isaiah 1 that we have been considering could well have come from the eighth-century BC setting of the prophetic ministry of Isaiah the son of Amoz in Jerusalem.[5] From what we otherwise know about the conditions of that age the reign of Uzziah in Jerusalem was one of prosperity in his small country of Judah. So too it appears were these years of prosperity in the related northern kingdom of Israel under the long and economically successful reign of Jeroboam II in Samaria. And yet for both countries all this, we can now see with the benefit of hindsight, was something of an end of the age, a *fin de siècle*. As far as the northern kingdom was concerned its nemesis was near, while for Judah the days of political independence would soon be ended. For both of these little nations this threat was due to the growing ambition and power of the Assyrian empire, in particular under the gifted leadership of Tiglath-pileser III. The fact is that henceforth these nations would be subject to the wills and needs of those able to muster enormous power, first the Assyrians, then later the Babylonians, then the Persians. Even later there would be Greek overlords, and then those of Rome – but that is to take us out of the time frame of the book of Isaiah and thus of our present concern.

A further factor for these nations seems to have been that by the eighth-century days of kings Uzziah of Judah and Jeroboam of Israel some internal domestic damage had taken place. Material prosperity had taken its toll of the souls of these nations, and while some members of the populace had grown rich, many – in all probability many, many more – seem to have been trampled upon and left behind in comparative penury. This is reflected in the utterances of the prophet Isaiah, some of which occur in the introductory chapter to the book (see, for example, 1.15, 17, 23.) In the not-dissimilar words of the prophet Amos we sense the same sorts of problems in the northern kingdom of Israel (see for example Amos 3.15; 4.1; 5.15, 24; 6.4–6). And as far as issues about the worship of Yahweh are concerned, it is clear from the book of the prophet Hosea that in those times there was much that was far from well in the kingdom of Israel (see Hosea 2.13; 4.12–14).

The contents of chapter 1 of Isaiah set forth what are some of the main issues to be dealt with in the rest of the book. Here are some of the ever-present issues that will be before those who are called to be the Lord's prophets. Thus here is the word spoken to those who have fallen away from the proper practice of their religion (1.2–3), the sickness of the body politic and religious (1.4–9), the ever-present temptation to abuse worship of the Lord, and the continuing call to seek the ways of justice and righteousness in communal life (1.10–17), that perpetual call to sinful people to amend their lives and turn to the Lord (1.18–20), what must be the Lord's sadness and distress over the need for judgement upon such evil and wrongdoing even though such judgement may be the means by which new life may come (1.21–26). That is, these are some of the themes that we shall find recurring in the book, though to these themes others will be added, these not infrequently coming out of, and reflecting, new situations that call for new and fresh words from various prophets. This we shall observe in this brief study.

Yet before go further into the book of Isaiah there is this also to say about the various themes that we have observed adumbrated in its opening chapter. These themes are in fact the ever-present issues for those who would live their lives in the faith and the ethical values of the Judaeo-Christian tradition. That is, for those who would live their lives in some sort of conformity with and faithfulness to the biblical tradition, here are some of the themes about which they must constantly be aware, and through such themes be guided to amend their lives accordingly, whether that be in directions that will lead to the divine pleasure, or whether that be to seek to avoid divine displeasure and judgement. Thus here are the timeless calls to religious people of every age to consider whether they have fallen away from the proper practice of their religion (1.2–3), or whether there is a deep and serious sickness in their communities (1.4–9), whether their worship is real and fervent or whether it has become an abuse of true worship, a mockery of what worship was and is intended to be (1.10–17). Here is the perpetual call to people to amend their lives (1.18–20), and the reminder of what deep sadness and anquish such unfaithfulness is to the Lord of all, yet what truly good possibilities for their lives in the future he offers to people (1.21–26).

All this is to say that here in the opening chapter of Isaiah are some of those vital words of scripture of which Jewish and Christian believers must ever be aware. Here is indeed divine guidance, direction, even censure, yet also hope, for the ongoing generations of believers, and surely even for those generations today. We shall come to see that such is to be found in material coming from many parts of the Isaiah book, but the point to be made at present is that it is here already in the first chapter. This is to say that what we are studying in the book of Isaiah is not merely an artefact of long ago merely of historical interest, but here rather is a written document that still has a word for us today, that is indeed sacred Scripture, a word that if we will but hear and receive it will surely come with power and hope, with challenge and reassurance, as 'the word of the Lord' to us.

It will not have escaped the notice of the attentive reader that I have made no mention of the closing verses of this chapter, namely 1.27–31. A large number of interpreters of the book of Isaiah judge that these verses come from a considerably later time than that of the prophet Isaiah of the eighth century.[6] The verses bear some of the hallmarks of apocalyptic literature, in which a final judgement is spoken about, as we shall come to see when we consider chapters 24 to 27, chapters that are expressed in this style of language. Yet the fact that we judge Isaiah 1.27–31 to come from a later time is in no way to denigrate its message or in any sense to set it on a level below that of the perceived 'authentic words' of Isaiah.[7] It, along with the words of Isaiah has been accepted into the canons of scripture of both Jews and Christians, and thereby has a right to be read and its message heard. These words come to us with the notes of both censure and encouragement, for they speak of the sure purposes of God, in particular that those divine purposes must in the end prevail, that what he wills will indeed be done. They remind us of the ultimate fates of both those who make themselves a part of those purposes and also of those who choose to live in opposition to them. Thus,

> Zion shall be redeemed by justice,
>   and those in her who repent, by righteousness.
> But rebels and sinners shall be destroyed together,
>   and those who forsake the Lord shall be consumed.
> (Isaiah 1.27–28)

No doubt some Christians who read these verses will make the familiar judgement that what is being spoken about here is the God of the Old Testament whose activity is so often characterised as judgemental whereas the God of the New Testament is a loving and saving God. While the Old Testament in some of its parts may indeed cause difficulties for Christians in their reading of it, we may at the same time very reasonably enquire just how much of the Old Testament is in reality like this. Further, we should recall that the note of judgement is also there in the New Testament. It is, for example, in the New Testament that we read the words, 'It is a fearful thing to fall into the hands of the living God' (Hebrews 10.31). Further, those twin futures that we are presented with in Isaiah 1.27–28, the judgement upon the sinners and the good life for the faithful, is there in John's gospel in those different responses to God's new presence and work through Jesus the Son. Thus the Jesus of St John's Gospel says,

> For God so loved the world that he gave his only Son, so that everyone who believes in him may not perish but may have eternal life. Indeed, God did not send the Son into the world to condemn the world, but in order that the world might be saved through him. Those who believe in him are not condemned; but those who do not believe are

condemned already, because they have not believed in the
name of the only Son of God. (John 3.16–18)

There is one more thing to say, and then we can move on from
chapter 1. It is to point out something that we have been doing
already and that we shall continue to do, namely to be looking at
and studying the book of Isaiah in two ways. The first of these
ways is that wherever possible we shall consider sections of the text
in the setting from which we think they came. But the crucial words
here are, 'wherever possible', because – as we have already seen –
we have to face the fact that frequently this is not possible. We cannot clearly see what the original setting was, and in such cases it is
perhaps best not to yield to the temptation to become too speculative. Yet if it is possible to be reasonably clear about the historical
setting from which a part of the text comes, then that must be of
great help to us in understanding what the writer, or the prophet,
or whoever, was trying to say, and why they were trying to say it.

The second way of understanding the book is to read it in the
larger parts into which it has been arranged, and indeed to read
the whole book as a complete work. Why did editors put the
whole work together? Presumably because they believed there
would be value and help for us in reading the whole book, and so
surely we should also seek to do that. Of course, we may then find
that whereas some piece of writing may originally have been
intended to convey a certain message, in the context of the whole
work it has come to bear a rather different message. There will
then be, maybe, two messages that we should be aware of, and
perhaps be ready to hear.[8] And on this basis we shall proceed,
and go on to the next part of the book of Isaiah.

Chapters 2 to 12: Judah and Jerusalem
Here begins the book proper, and the subject and concern is the
prophet's home country of Judah and, most importantly, its capital city Jerusalem. Later, as we shall see, the subjects of the
prophet's concerns (which he says are the concerns of God) will,
so to speak, go outwards in ever-widening circles, moving away

from the more 'domestic' political and religious concerns to the international, and then – most boldly – to what we might call the cosmic. While this is to anticipate what will be spoken about in the following pages, it is mentioned here by way of illustration of the fact that the book of Isaiah is far more than a mere random collection of words, oracles, messages, but rather that there is a shape, an order, a coherence, a real sense of logic about the whole work. In the meantime, we are invited to consider the situation in Judah and Jerusalem in the eighth century BC, and some later ages, through the eyes of, and with the concerns of, the prophet Isaiah and others – and their God, and ours.

As was the case with chapter 1 of the book, so here with these chapters we can hardly escape the conclusion that they have been carefully and purposefully put together, and, moreover, at a time later than that of the prophet Isaiah. In the first place there is a definite beginning to this section, this being observed with the new word of introduction in 2.1, and in the second place with the definite conclusion to it in the liturgical hymn of praise of chapter 12. However, the varied contents of these chapters are not in the logical or chronological order that we might have expected. For instance, this whole block of material after opening with the renewed introductory superscription in 2.1, goes on in 2.2–5 to paint a grandiose picture of Jerusalem as the city and centre to which the nations stream in order that they may learn of the ways and will of the God of Israel. Here also will they learn the ways of peace between the nations, of the situation where swords will have been beaten into ploughshares and where the arts and strategies of war will no longer be needed. Much of the prophecy in 2.2–4 is to be found also in the book of the prophet Micah (Micah 4.1–4), and it certainly reads like a resounding expression of hope and confidence for the future. It is a somewhat idealised picture of the future glory and greatness of Jerusalem that is generally regarded as coming from a later time from that of Isaiah's ministry in the eighth century. Yet we can surely understand that it has been placed at the beginning of this large block of material about Judah and Jerusalem so as to make a bold and confident statement about the glorious possibilities that there are in the purposes of God for the city of Jerusalem. Meanwhile, what great need there is for God's own people, here as often in the book of Isaiah called 'house of Jacob' (that is, the people who are descended from the patriarch Jacob), to walk humbly in the light of the Lord so that they may do their part to progressing towards the fulfilment of the vision. This thought – this plea – is expressed in Isaiah 2.5, a verse that is not found in the version of this oracle in Micah.

> O house of Jacob,
>   come, let us walk
>   in the light of the Lord! (Isaiah 2.5)

It may be that the insertion of these words into the beginning of the Isaiah 2–12 block of material was intended not only to give a glorious vision of the peaceful and hopeful kingdoms, but also – and how important that this should be expressed at the beginning of the section! – that a vital part of the realisation of this vision glorious must lie with the people of God, the people of Jacob. That is, that they take care to walk in the light of the Lord.

Then straight after that we are thrown into a series of prophecies concerning the grim reality of contemporary life in Jerusalem. This is what the city is like at a particular historical moment, and here is a place that cannot but be under divine condemnation and judgement, a judgement that will now be spoken about. For the fact is that so much in this city is plain contrary to what the Lord wills, what he has ordained should prevail and be found there. There are proud people whose reliance is upon themselves and upon their worldly possessions, and not in the Holy One of Israel (2.6–22). The rulers of the city are condemned (3.13–15), and so too are the proud, wealthy women (3.16–24). A sombre fate awaits these women (3.25—4.1), itself something of a reflection of the coming fate of the whole city (3.1–12).

Yet in the midst of these sombre and chilling words of divine condemnation and judgement, there break out words of comfort, and expressions of hope. However, this particular promise of hope is not so much for the whole community of people and city, but rather for just a small remnant of them, a theme to which the prophet Isaiah will return, and to which another prophet who words are recorded in the book will develop. The remnant theme in the book of Isaiah has its first airing here in 4.2–6.

> On that day the branch of the Lord shall be beautiful and glorious, and the fruit of the land shall be the pride and glory of the survivors of Israel. (Isaiah 4.2)

In all probability this oracle comes from a later time from that of Isaiah,[9] but its placement here is entirely appropriate, for it makes clear that while the city of Jerusalem may be sinful and depraved, far removed in life and spirit from what the Lord intended, yet in God is there hope for the future. This will be made possible through a remnant, through the survival and faithfulness of a small group out of the original whole. Here is a further evidence of the editorial processes that contributed to the book of Isaiah that we now have.

We have already seen that the book opens with the complaint that the Lord God has with his people (1.2–3), and this 'complaint theme' is expressed in the prophet's 'Song of the Vineyard', found in 5.1–7, and to which we now turn. We are to imagine the 'song' being 'sung' by the prophet, and in it he bewails the grim situation of his 'friend' (or 'beloved' in NRSV) who turns out to be none other than God, the one who did everything reasonably possible to ensure that the vineyard would be in such good shape that it could be confidently expected to bear good fruit. Alas, it was not fruitful at all!

> Let me sing for my beloved
>   my love-song concerning his vineyard:
> My beloved had a vineyard
>   on a very fertile hill.
> He dug it and cleared it of stones,
>   and planted it with choice vines;
> he built a watch-tower in the midst of it,
>   and hewed out a wine vat in it;

> he expected it to yield grapes,
>   but it yielded wild grapes. (Isaiah 5.1–2)

The reader is invited to enter into this matter of the grave disappointment suffered by the owner of the vineyard (5.3–4), and is then told what the owner (God) is going to do, namely destroy and abandon it (5.5–6). Finally, in verse 7 all is revealed, and the meaning of the song – in fact it turns out to be a parable rather like Nathan's in 2 Samuel 12.1–4 – is explained in some detail. Thus:

> For the vineyard of the Lord of hosts
>   is the house of Israel,
> and the people of Judah
>   are his pleasant planting;
> he expected justice,
>   but saw bloodshed;
> righteousness,
>   but heard a cry! (Isaiah 5.7)

Here truly is the basic message of the eighth-century prophet Isaiah: it is about God having chosen his people Israel to be his 'vineyard', and having lavished upon them devoted attention, they have failed to bring forth the intended and desired fruit. What here makes its appearance once again is the social critique of the prophet. True religion for the prophet and his God is not to do merely with belief in God, trust in God, prayer and praise, but it is to embrace a much wider spectrum of life. Though the word is modern, and anachronistic as regards Isaiah, the fact is that the prophet yearned for his people to have a spirituality that embraced justice in personal relationships, and righteousness in the life of society, that is the love of neighbour as the vital concomitant of prayer and praise. What we find expressed here in Isaiah's parable of the vineyard is the depth of anger and disappointment on the part of God as a result of the sin and failure of those very people called to be in a most especial way his people. True, there is nothing here, as has been pointed out, about forgiveness, restoration, redemption, but before we are

finished with our study of the book of Isaiah we shall have dis-
covered that there is more to be said about the whole matter
than we find here.[10]

Yet as far as the eighth-century BC situation in Jerusalem and
Judah was concerned the message of Isaiah had to be that of the
anger of the Lord (9.8–21; 5.25–30). The prophet felt a divine
compulsion to proclaim a dreadful message about the judgement
of God not only to his fellow people, but also in a special and particular way to those upon whom the leadership of those people
had been entrusted. If anything, theirs was the greater sin
(10.1–4a; 5.8–24).

Nevertheless, hard on the heels of this message of searing
divine judgement upon the people of Judah and Jerusalem, and
their leaders, comes something very different, the vision of the
mighty Lord of all, yet the Lord who has plans and purposes for
his people, and who in this mighty epiphany makes his call to
Isaiah, the son of Amoz, to be his prophet. Here in Isaiah chapter 6 is one of the truly great passages in the whole of the Old
Testament, and it is great and profound because it is about the
living God who is the Lord of all and also the Holy one of Israel.

But first, a brief word about the setting in the book of Isaiah
occupied by this remarkable passage. With Isaiah 6 there begins
a definite section within the larger unit comprising chapters 2 to
12. For Isaiah 6.1–13 is followed by a series of prophetic oracles
about the Syro-Ephraimite war (7.1–8.22), and there are certain
clues to suggest that chapter 6 has been intentionally written up
in the light of the experiences of the Syro-Ephraimite war, so as
to serve as a prelude to the oracles about the war. Some of these
details will emerge as we proceed. This is not in any way at all to
denigrate this chapter, but it is to observe that in the writing of it
attention has been given to its wider setting, that its themes –
God, his prophet, and his people – have been given particular
emphases that will serve to illuminate the political and religious
follies displayed in the Syro-Ephraimite war, and to point to
where the real help for the nation, its individual people, and its
leaders is to be found.

Isaiah chapter 6 takes us in vision into the world of God, yet is a vision seen on earth, apparently in the Jerusalem temple (see 6.4). J. Blenkinsopp entitles this chapter 'The Throne Room Vision',[11] and such indeed it is:

> In the year that King Uzziah died, I saw the Lord sitting on a throne, high and lofty; and the hem of his robe filled the temple. Seraphs were in attendance above him; each had six wings: with two they covered their faces, and with two they covered their feet, and with two they flew. And one called to another and said:
> 'Holy, holy, holy is the Lord of hosts;
> the whole earth is full of his glory.' (Isaiah 6.1–3)

Time and again it has been pointed out that there are three movements in the account of this remarkable scene. The first is quite simply – but utterly remarkable – that the man Isaiah had this experience of God. For the fact is that the one who reveals himself to Isaiah is an exalted and transcendent being, the one whose abode in not on the earth, whose throne is so high and lofty, the mere hem of whose robe is voluminous, (v. 1), who is attended by the semi-divine beings (seraphs) who though they appear to dwell near this mighty one are themselves conscious of his otherness to themselves, his holiness, and who thus both veil their faces before him (v. 2), and ceaselessly utter their expressions of praise and worship (v. 3).

All this is to say that in these verses we are being introduced to a very exalted Lord who while he does make his appearance to Isaiah is himself the Lord of worlds far away. This is the Lord God we are constantly reading about, and being told about, in the book of Isaiah. Here is the Lord of his chosen people (ch. 2–12), but the Lord also of many nations (ch. 13–23), the Lord even of all ages and time (ch. 24–27), who has mighty creating and creative powers (ch. 40), who will not share his glory with another (ch. 45, 46), who has plans and purposes for his people (ch. 41).

The second movement in this chapter speaks of the sense of unworthiness of the man who is the recipient of this vision, and of his appreciation of the fact that he is bound up in the bundle of a humanity that is sinful and unworthy (6.4–5). Thus the prophet's sense of wonder and rapture grows, for in spite of human sin and failure the purposes of the Lord yet prevail and his loving care for his people continues.

Then the third movement is the call of this sinful person, who having received symbolic forgiveness, is enlisted in the divine service, and who will be sent by God and who will go for him (vv. 6–8). And strange indeed will be his work (vv. 9–12), apparently to stop the ears and close the eyes of people already blind and deaf to the Lord's will! This has been understood in various ways, either that the message of doom for the people was intended to be 'a concrete expression of the divine will',[12] or that this represents the great judgement upon those to whom so much was promised and who in their responses have failed so dismally,[13] or that this is speaking of the most radical renewal that must take place for God's people, a renewal that will only come about in the rebirth following death.[14] Yet out of all this burning, as if by a miracle, will come new life, a veritable phoenix arising from the ashes (v. 13).

So to chapters 7 and 8. In about the year 734 BC a coalition of Syria, otherwise known in the Old Testament as Aram, and the northern kingdom of Israel, otherwise known in the Old Testament as Ephraim – thus the 'Syro-Ephraimite' coalition causing the 'Syro-Ephraimite' war – laid siege to Jerusalem with, it seems, the intention of putting their own nominee on the throne there, a certain 'son of Tabeel', of whom we know nothing else (Isaiah 7.1–6).[15] Through the account of this incident in these chapters we are being taken into a wider world than that merely of Judah and Jerusalem. This is a tendency that we shall see continuing as we proceed through the book: that in thought we are invited to go progressively into ever-widening realms of the purposes of God in the world. Here is the first step into that world that lay beyond the world of Judah and Jerusalem, and here we read of different reactions on the parts of the various individuals and groups who are caught up in, or affected by, or being confronted by, this 'international' incident.

One reaction to these events – and according to the record in the Isaiah book this does seem to have been a fairly widespread reaction – was the one of panic. In Isaiah 7.2 we read, 'When the house of David heard that Aram had allied itself with Ephraim, the heart of Ahaz and the heart of his people shook as the trees of the forest shake before the wind.' Yet for the prophet Isaiah there was little cause for panic, but rather his command from the Lord was to say to the king:

> Take heed, be quiet, do not fear, and do not let your heart be faint because of these two smouldering stumps of fire-brands, because of the fierce anger of Rezin and Aram and the son of Remaliah. (Isaiah 7.4)

What Isaiah counselled Ahaz to do was to place his trust fairly and squarely in the Lord, warning him that without such trust he would not be able to stand.

> If you do not stand firm in faith,
> you shall not stand at all. (Isaiah 7.9)

There has been much discussion as to what Isaiah intended through this word, and in particular what he thought the king should do, or should not do, in the political and military aspects of the incident. Did the prophet intend, perhaps, that if the king really trusted in God then he would not need to make any military decisions and dispositions? Was the prophet saying anything here about appealing, or not appealing, to Assyria for military help? My own judgement is that what Isaiah was talking about here was the religious foundation of faith and trust in God that the king needed to have as a basis for, a foundation upon which he could build as he made his necessary political decisions and his also-necessary military dispositions. [16]

Another much-discussed verse that occurs in this account of the Syro-Ephraimite war is Isaiah 7.14, which speaks of the famous sign of Immanuel. The situation is that the prophet has offered to give the king a sign – any sign that he cares to choose – from God, and this by way of guidance and help to the king in this difficult situation in which he finds himself. But Ahaz – assuming, it would appear, a mantle of piety – says he does not want a sign because he does not wish to put God to the test. The response of Isaiah was that whether or not the king wants a sign, he is getting one. However, it has to be said that what he got was a most enigmatic sign. Was it any clearer to Ahaz than it has been to generations of readers, hearers and scholars since then? This was the sign:

> Therefore the Lord himself will give you a sign. Look, the young woman is with child and shall bear a son, and shall name him Immanuel. (Isaiah 7.14)

We cannot deal here with all the ramifications of the meaning of this sign, [17] but it may well be that through these words and those of the verses that follow we are to understand that what the prophet was giving to Ahaz was a double sign. That is, it was intended both to warn him and also to give him hope. It was a warning of the Lord's judgement upon his people because of their lack of faith in him (see 7.17, 18–25; 8.5–8, 19–22), but it was also hopeful in that in the longer term things would turn out better for Judah and Jerusalem (see 7.16; 8.1–4, 9–10).

There is a further expression of hope here in the talk about remnant. Something in this regard is being expressed through the name of the child that Isaiah is told to take with him on his mission to speak with King Ahaz, his young son Shear-jashub, his name meaning literally 'A Remnant shall Return' (see 7.3). We can also catch a glimpse of this theme in what we are told about the small group of believing ones whom the prophet gathers around him in this time of national crisis (8.16–18), and it is also there in the chapter about Isaiah's vision of God (6.13). This is one of the clues that suggests to us that chapter 6 has been composed in such a way that it does stand in a particular relationship with chapters 7 and 8: it brings out various themes that are also to be found in them. Another of the themes common to chapter 6 and chapters 7 to 8 is that of hardness of heart towards God.

This is spoken about in 6.9–12 regarding the people in general, and of Ahaz in 7.12. Further there is the threat of the devastation of the land both in 6.11–13 and also in 7.17, 18–25; 8.19–22. Yet beyond such devastation there can under God be hope for the future, as 6.13 indicates.

Yet there is more to come on this subject of new life, and for this we turn to chapter 9. This chapter is prefaced by an introductory verse (9.1) which appears to have been placed here so that the words that follow are understood to have an application in the situation of gloom and despondency for the old kingdom of Israel (Ephraim) in the miserable aftermath of the Syro-Ephraimite war ('In the former time he brought into contempt the land of Zebulun and the land of Naphtali ...'). But then with 9.2 there begin thrilling words about a future ruler – truly, a God-given ruler – through whose good and wise rule new life will come for the people of Israel. As we read this passage we need to bear in mind that the prophet was sure that in the Syro-Ephraimite war his people had been poorly led, so much so that he had harsh things to say about the Judean king Ahaz (see for example 7.13). When it came to the king of the northern kingdom of Israel, Isaiah did not deign to address him by his name, but instead, as if slightingly, referred to him as 'the son of Remaliah' (7.5; compare 2 Kings 16.1). Yet what hope there is now! Here in 9.2–7 we are told that through the birth of a child who will come to occupy the historic throne of David new and good times will dawn. See what glorious and exalted titles will be his:

> For a child has been born for us,
>   a son given to us;
> authority rests upon his shoulders;
>   and he is named
> Wonderful Counsellor, Mighty God,
>   Everlasting Father, Prince of Peace. (Isaiah 9.6)

Moreover, how differently will he rule when compared with some kings in the past. There will, for example, be a new spirit of justice abroad (compare 1.26–27):

His authority shall grow continually,
and there shall be endless peace
for the throne of David and his kingdom.
He will establish and uphold it
with justice and with righteousness
from this time onwards and for evermore. (Isaiah 9.7)

A further vision of hope attaching to a coming national ruler who will profoundly transform situations is found in Isaiah 11.1–9, and again the emphasis is on wise and good leadership and statecraft (11.1–2). Through the rule of this king, justice and righteousness will prevail (11.3–5), with the result that there will be peace and true godliness in the land (11.6–9).

Who is this king? Or, maybe, who are these kings? Some argue that the king in view in the first (9.2–7) of these passages is the good King Hezekiah, the son of the somewhat worthless Ahaz. Stacey in his commentary on Isaiah 1–39 mentions the suggestion that this passage was perhaps composed to mark the accession of a king, perhaps indeed Hezekiah.[18] My own view is that both of these passages are intended to be portrayals of an ideal of king-ship. They do not have in mind any particular historic king, but are, rather, longing expressions for the coming one day of the ideal king who will bring peace and justice, and much else beside.[19] At any rate what we find set out here in 9.2–7 and 11.1–9 are visions of what good and true kingship is. They are portrayals of the ideal leadership of the people – and how blest are the people when they have leaders such as these!

While we are on this subject of kingship, there is one other king to be spoken about, one who also makes his appearance in this part of the book of Isaiah. Here again we are being invited in thought to take yet another step into the wider world, for this fur-ther king is none other than the king of Assyria. The first reference to him in the book of Isaiah is decidedly brief and allusive. In Isaiah 7.17 we have the prophet's warning to his people of the coming judgement of God, brought about because of their lack of faith and trust in God as they are threatened by the two petty and rather impotent kings of Israel and Syria (see 7.4!). Be warned, Isaiah seems to be saying to the people: instead of your being threatened by these very minor kings, you will soon know a real threat, nothing less than the might and authority of a proper king – the king of Assyria. The theme, however, receives more expansive treatment in Isaiah 10.5–11, a passage that begins with the Lord speaking (through his prophet) of 'Assyria, the rod of my anger' (10.5). That is, the king of Assyria is portrayed as being the one appointed by the Lord to put his judgement of his people into worldly effect. The king of Assyria, however, is not himself aware of this particular calling that he has: rather, his warlike actions are dictated by his personal considerations and his own agenda. Thus,

> but it is in his heart to destroy,
> and to cut off nations not a few. (Isaiah 10.7b)

And thus – and again the king of Assyria is in blissful ignorance of it – a grim fate awaits this man who in his God-given task has vastly overstepped the mark. Hence for this tyrant,

> When the Lord has finished all his work on Mount Zion
> and on Jerusalem, he will punish the arrogant boasting of
> the king of Assyria and his haughty pride. (Isaiah 10.12)

And that, for the time being, is perhaps enough about kings in the book of Isaiah – but there will be more later. Other kings of the great nations will make their appearances, not only King Sennacherib of Assyria (ch. 36–37) and King Merodach-baladan son of Baladan of Babylon (ch. 39), but also the Persian king Cyrus referred to by the Second Isaiah as the Lord's shepherd (44.28), whose right hand the Lord has grasped with the purpose of subduing nations and setting his own people free (45.1–7). Further, as we proceed through the book of Isaiah we shall need to address the question why it is that in later parts of the book we hear no more about Israelite kings whereas talk of servants comes very clearly into focus. But that is for later. [20]

Meanwhile, to return to chapter 10, there is talk of the advance of an enemy (10.27b–32), though the book does not name the enemy. The result of this is that Isaiah scholarship has found here a happy hunting ground,[21] but for our present purposes we can be content to remain in ignorance as to the identity of this enemy. Then in 10.33–34 there follows talk of the Lord of hosts cutting down tall trees, but once again the details elude us. To what, to whom do these trees refer? Is this reference to God's judgement on Judah and Jerusalem, or alternatively on Assyria? Again, we have to hold our hands up and say that we do not know.

Yet, even in this setting of trees coming tumbling down, and boughs being lopped with terrifying power (10.33), the theme of hope once more makes its appearance. Amidst crisis and judgement there is hope in the long term for Zion (Jerusalem) (10.24–27a), and there is hope in a remnant (10.20–23). Here is the reappearance of what we have already seen is one of the prophet's themes in this period of his ministry. Yet here there is even more than hope in a small remnant, for here is an expression of hope of full restoration (11.10–16). Part of this grandiose expression of hope is cast in 'exodus' language, a form of speech that shall see recurring in chapters 40 to 55 (for example in 41.8–20). That is, as in the past, so we read in the book of Exodus, God led his people out of the harshness of life in Egypt, so once again will he bring them back home, in 11.10–16 from Assyria, and in chapters 40 to 55 from Babylon. Thus,

> So there shall be a highway from Assyria
>   for the remnant that is left of his people,
> as there was for Israel
>   when they came up from the land of Egypt.
> (Isaiah 11.16)

So we come to the short chapter 12, a piece which makes a conclusion to the oracles in chapters 2 to 12, and which at the same time serves as an interlude before the block of material contained in chapters 13 to 23 which follows. This chapter is made up of two brief hymns of praise, both expressed in the language of the biblical psalms. The first of these is in verses 1–2, and is in

the form of an individual thanksgiving, while the second, in verses 3–6, is like a communal thanksgiving.[22] In verse 2 it will be
observed that the word 'salvation' appears twice, in each case
being a play in Hebrew on the name 'Isaiah'. Yet both of these
mini-psalms of thanksgiving provide a satisfying conclusion to
what has gone before. While they do not anticipate what is to
come in the following chapters, they do perhaps serve to suggest
that those past times of divine judgement and such badly flawed
human leadership are past, and that now God's people can give
him their thanks that they have been safely and successfully delivered from their enemies.

Before we leave chapter 12 we should briefly take note of two
matters, both relevant to our particular concern. In the first place,
it is widely considered that the author here is not Isaiah. It is not
his style, his language or his characteristic ideas that are found in
these verses. Rather, what we have here is 'a patchwork of biblical citations and allusions',[23] in particular from the book of
Psalms (Psalms 118.21; 88.22; 25.5; 118.14; 105.1; 148.13; 9.12;
30.50). That is, here once again it looks as if we are observing the
hand and the work of an editor or various editors. This is surely
a deliberate piece of editorial activity intended to close off these
early chapters of the book, to bring them to a satisfactory and satisfying conclusion.

In the second place we should take note of the fact that the
composition of this chapter is in the form of a thanksgiving, and
that as we continue to work through the Isaiah book we shall
come across other such 'liturgical' compositions. That is, we have
here material that looks as if it was intended for the activity of the
worship of God. At least it has the appearance and form of that
type of written material. We shall come across other pieces in the
book of Isaiah that bear this impression of being worship, or at
least worship-like, materials, particularly in chapter 33, and in a
significant number of places in chapters 40 to 55.

Chapters 13 to 23: Into the wider world

These chapters take us into a much wider world than hitherto we have been concerned with in the book of Isaiah. In chapters 7 and 8 we were invited to reflect upon the Syro-Ephraimite war and its aftermath, and to see in those events a number of things – human sinfulness, political inadequacy and lack of wisdom, the purposes of God as he is portrayed as working his works through the agency of foreign nations, speaking his word to his people through his prophets, and preserving at least a remnant of those people so that his work in the world through them may continue. Now we are taken in thought to places which geographically are much further afield. Here we read prophetic words concerning a number of other nations and peoples: Babylon (13.1–22; 14.3–23; 21.1–10), Philistia (14.29–31), Moab (15.1—16.14), Damascus (17.1–3), Ethiopia (18.1–7), Egypt (19.1–17), Edom (21.11–12), Kedarite Arabs (21.13–17), and Phoenician cities (23.1–18).

Oracles such as these are generally called 'oracles against the nations', and we come across collections of them in other biblical books of the prophets: Amos 1.3—2.3; Jeremiah 46—51; Ezekiel 25—32. However, we do not know what was the intended significance of these oracles at the times when they were originally composed and uttered. We have no records of any of the prophets going to such nations, venturing on 'preaching missions' to them, and nor do we have any evidence to suggest that the leaders and peoples of such nations had any knowledge of what these various Hebrew prophets had to say about them. [24]

If, then, we do not think that these oracles were in any intentional way proclaimed to any of the various rulers and peoples spoken about in them, what are we to say as regards the purpose of them? In all probability this was bound up with a concern to make it clear – and this in the first place to the people of Judah and Jerusalem – that the Lord God of Israel is the God of much more than merely Israel. That is, the 'Holy One of Israel', as this God is frequently called in the book of Isaiah, as well as having a particular relationship with the people of Israel, Jacob, is also the Lord of all the world. He is Lord of the Assyrians (see Isaiah

10.1–19), though indeed those people may not be aware of that fact. He is Lord of the Babylonians, as we shall come to see, and most definitely he is Lord of the Persians who swallowed up the Babylonian empire. In particular the Lord was at work, working out his purposes in the sixth century BC, through the Persian ruler Cyrus. Cyrus may not have been aware of this fact, but the book of Isaiah avers that he had been called by the Lord for this very purpose, and was being used so as to give earthly effect to the plans that God had for his people who were at that time living as exiles in Babylon (44.28—45.7).

Moreover, this concern that the Holy One of Israel is the Lord of all nations extends to the issue of what is right and what is wrong in the life of nations. That is, an issue lying behind these oracles against the nations is concern over morality in the world. Is the world a moral place? If Yahweh shows himself holy by his righteousness (that is, he demonstrates his difference from us in the ways in which he acts, in goodness and justice, in ways that will result in conditions of righteousness: see Isaiah 5.16), and if he is also a God of power and strength, then he must have something to say about – and sometimes even things to do about – situations of grave immorality within nations, and in the dealings that go on between nations.

Thus there are foreign nations spoken about in Isaiah 13 to 23 whose conduct is portrayed as being particularly heinous, and, to be sure, these receive sharp words of judgement, and in some cases warnings of coming doom. Yet we should not think that all the judgement in these chapters is directed against the foreign nations. Far from it. Rather, not only do we find here that Israel itself is at times under condemnation, but at the same time here are thrilling passages that speak of nations coming to be united, and of nations coming to acknowledge the lordship of the Holy One of Israel. David Stacey in his commentary on Isaiah 1 to 39 has some helpful words about these chapters. Having said that the content of them must be faced, he goes on to say:

> Terrible calamities do happen, arrogance and wickedness

still abound, theists believe in a moral ordering of the universe and also maintain that God is absolutely sovereign. In these chapters the book of Isaiah tries to hold these four factors together. We may not be fully satisfied with the result, but we can scarcely claim that we have nothing to learn from the approach. [25]

A study of these chapters with the help of a scholarly commentary will make clear that many questions remain unresolved regarding the historical setting and authorship of a large number of the individual oracles. The fact is that the prophetic words here – in the main words concerned with Israel's surrounding nations – have been gathered together on a thematic rather than historical basis. Further, we find that the various parts of these chapters appear to come from widely different dates, and even eras.

We should also take notice of and acknowledge a remarkable boldness of thought in Isaiah 13 to 23, for while in worldly terms nations like Assyria, Babylonia, Egypt did command in comparison with Israel and Judah quite overwhelming power and authority, yet even so within these chapters their fate can be spoken about either as historical fact or in confident expectation. However, in no way is the thought that they are liable to be defeated by tiny Judah and Jerusalem – and certainly Judah and Jerusalem should not be possessed of such misguided confidence and pride in its own power and abilities! – but the confident assurance is that great though their might is, yet greater by far is the might of Yahweh, the Holy One of Israel. Thus we read of the fall of Assyria (14.24–27; 17.12–14), of the fate of Babylon (13.1–22; 14.1–23; 17.12–14; 21.1–10), of the downfall of Egypt and Ethiopia (19.1–5; 18.1–7; 20.1–6). Even Tyre (23.1–18), perhaps regarded in Israel and Judah's region as the nation without peer or rival in regard to glory and success, is spoken about here as being due very soon to perish. It has been suggested that it is this apparent, and worldly, peerlessness of Tyre (Phoenicia) which has led to this oracle being placed at the end of the whole series, at its climax. [26]

Thus the central point and theme in these chapters is that although in worldly terms these nations may have great power and might, yet *the* supreme power and might in all the world belongs to the Lord God of Israel. Yet also condemned are the smaller players, the smaller nations, such as the people of Arabia (21.11–17), the Philistines (14.28–32), Israel's old enemy (yet at times friend in need, as portrayed, for instance, in the book of Ruth) Moab (15.1—16.14), Damascus and Israel (17.1–11). And also mentioned here as standing in immediate danger of condemnation are certain individuals in Jerusalem (22.1–14, 15–25).

Yet not everything in these chapters is condemnatory, for here also is a remarkable vision of the worship of Yahweh in Egypt (19.16–25), something both of a bold promise of good things to come, yet perhaps also having within it some realistic reflection of an existing practice, for we do hear of a temple established for Yahweh worship in Leontopolis in Upper Egypt,[27] and of Yahweh worship taking place at the Egyptian Jewish colony at Elephantine.[28] And that historical note provides a suitable transition for us into the next block of material in the book of Isaiah. This is chapters 24 to 27, and it will take us into a very great and extensive historical context.

Chapters 24 to 27: The context of history

While chapters 13 to 23 took us into the wider world of the nations, chapters 24 to 27 invite us to look into the future, to consider a long and forward-looking historical frame. That is, while chapters 13 to 23 affirm that the purposes of Yahweh are not confined to the little territories of Israel and Judah, and their immediately surrounding areas and nations, so chapters 24 to 27 make their own affirmation that those divine purposes are not just for the immediate age but that they will find their fulfilment in a much longer time span, one, as we shall see, that may even encroach upon the 'end time' of human history. This is what is known as eschatology, and this is to say that Isaiah 24 to 27 is dominated by eschatological ('end time') thought, and that the predominant theme of these chapters concerns the issue of where the whole historical process is going, what it is moving towards.

That is something about the general thrust, the general *tendenz*, of these chapters, but there is also this to be said. A certain amount of this material is expressed in apocalyptic language. Apocalyptic language, and the thought that lay behind the use of this sort of language, came to its zenith between about 200 BC and AD 100, and was concerned to express 'revelations' (what the word 'apocalyptic' means) about the end of the present world order and the divine bringing-in of a new era and order of good things. The two main examples of this literature in the Bible are parts of the books of Daniel and Revelation, but we also find in various other parts of the Old Testament a form and style of writing that is in the developmental stage of apocalyptic writing, what with further development will issue in full-blooded apocalyptic thought. The literature from this developing stage is sometimes called proto-apocalyptic, and amongst other places we find examples of it in the book of Isaiah, first in chapters 24 to 27 (these chapters sometimes being called 'The Great Apocalypse') and then also in chapters 34 to 35 (this sometimes being called 'The Little Apocalypse').[29]

However, already in Isaiah 24 to 27 there is to be observed the principal characteristic of this apocalyptic material, namely the looking forward to the rule of God in the world (see, for example, 24.23), but that this is envisaged as taking place in a much more extreme and cataclysmic way than is generally to be found in the prophetic literature. For example, the incoming of the reign of God in Isaiah 24.21–23 and 25.6–10a is expressed and portrayed in rather more dramatic ways than is the new order set forth in the more traditional prophetical language in, say, Amos 9.11–15. How gentle, how pastoral does the latter appear in comparison with the former in its talk about punishment, prisons and prisoners, effects or reflections being experienced even in the sun and the moon (Isaiah 24.21–23). Such is the style of apocalyptic literature. To be sure, it is not a matter of everything in Isaiah 24 to 27 being expressed in this apocalyptic language, but parts of it are. Thus here is talk of the imprisonment of earthly powers and authorities (24.22), the abolition of death (25.8), and one of the Old Testament's very few references to the resurrection of the dead (26.19). Here, as well as talk of the present sufferings of creation (24.16b), we also read of the joy of God's coming end-time banquet (25.6–10a).

Christopher Seitz in his commentary on Isaiah 1 to 39 has entitled chapters 24 to 27 'A Tale of Two Cities',[30] and this is a helpful way of gaining an overview of this block of material. For here portrayed on the one hand is a city that is evil, a city whose deeds are evil, but which is not named (24.10, 12; 25.2–3; 26.5; 27.10). How are we to explain this anonymity, and what city is perhaps intended? It may be that what we are to understand is that here is a general, intentionally generalised, message of judgement upon any and all cities that are evil, and that this has been deliberately expressed so as to give a timelessness to the message of divine judgement. If the message had been made more specific, dealing with one particular city at a given historical moment, and if that city had, let us say, fallen to its enemies, then it might have been felt that now that evil place and its people had received the deserved judgement, that thereby the prophecy had been spent, it had been fulfilled. Rather instead, by generalising the matter the issue was lifted out of the world's historical time frame and thereby the message has been given a whole new and on-going lease of life, a long-lasting significance, ever there for those who have ears to hear and eyes to see that the judgement of the Lord is ever and always, and everywhere, upon sinful cities, upon their inhabitants, and above all upon their leaders.

Naturally, it could well be that some of the oracles included in these chapters were once concerned with particular cities, quite probably some of the cities spoken about in the oracles against the nations now gathered together in chapters 13 to 23. Further, it is highly probable that though the name Babylon does not occur in Isaiah 24 to 27, yet this is the city that the editors of the final redaction of these four chapters had in their minds. It is widely thought that these chapters were fashioned into their final and present form in the time of Babylonian domination over Judah, Jerusalem and elsewhere, that is in the sixth century BC, in the period of the exile of Israelite people in Babylon, and before the conquests of Cyrus the Persian ruler, through which life would change in such remarkable ways for these and other people. That new situation is surely the one that is reflected in the thrilling chapters 40 to 55 of the book of Isaiah.

But to return to the judgement upon the sinful city, this is spoken about in confident tone to the effect that it will surely be brought about by the Lord, the Lord who hears the cries of those who suffer, and who through his actions comes to be revered and feared by saints and sinners alike. Thus,

> O Lord, you are my God;
>> I will exalt you, I will praise your name;
> for you have done wonderful things,
>> plans formed of old, faithful and sure.
> For you have made the city a heap,
>> the fortified city a ruin;
> the palace of aliens is a city no more,
>> it will never be rebuilt.
> Therefore strong peoples will glorify you;
>> cities of ruthless nations will fear you.
> For you have been a refuge to the poor,
>> a refuge to the needy in their distress,
>> a shelter from the rainstorm and a shade from
>>> the heat.
> When the blast of the ruthless was like a winter
>> rainstorm,
>> the noise of aliens like heat in a dry place,
> you subdued the heat with the shade of clouds;
>> the song of the ruthless was stilled. (Isaiah 25.1–5)

Then also there is the promise of a city whose life and nature will be of a totally new order of things. Thus,

> On that day this song will be sung in the land of Judah:

> We have a strong city;
> > he sets up victory
> > like walls and bulwarks.
> Open the gates,
> > so that the righteous nation that keeps faith
> > may enter in.
> Those of steadfast mind you keep in peace –
> > in peace because they trust in you.
> Trust in the Lord for ever,
> > for in the Lord God
> > you have an everlasting rock. (Isaiah 26.1–4)

The grand result of all this will be a land of godliness and prosperity. Of particular mention here is the assurance of a good and productive vineyard, symbolic of course of the bringing forth of good and productive things in the lives of the nations and in their leaders and peoples. We recognise here the imagery of Isaiah 5.1–7 being taken up and being given a new application for a later and different situation. This reapplication of earlier themes and words we have already observed is a characteristic feature of the book of Isaiah.

> On that day:
> A pleasant vineyard, sing about it!
> > I, the Lord, am its keeper;
> > every moment I water it.
> I guard it night and day
> > so that no one can harm it;
> > I have no wrath.
> If it gives me thorns and briers,
> > I will march to battle against it.
> > I will burn it up.
> Or else let it cling to me for protection,
> > let it make peace with me,
> > let it make peace with me. (Isaiah 27.2–5)

What is being contrasted here is a present world order dominated by the standards and mores of the human order, with the some-day to be attained new and God-given order of things in which harmony, peace and order, justice, goodness and righteousness abound. Thus here, not only is there the sharp contrast drawn between present sinful states with their cities, and a new and bright beneficent order under God, but there is also the contrast between high fortifications, made necessary because of the pride and ambition for further territory of Moab, a pride and ambition which will now be brought down low, even to the dust (25.12), and that mountain where God prepares a feast for all peoples (25.6–9), that banquet that will leave people so gladly rejoicing in the Lord's salvation (25.9).

Before we leave this passage we do well to take note of one further detail. In 27.4 we have a reference to 'thorns and briers', an expression we have already come across in a number of places, 5.6; 7.23, 24, 25; 9.18; 10.17. In all of these occurrences the same two words are used for 'briers' and 'thorns', and further, neither of these words occur elsewhere in the Old Testament. In Isaiah 32.13 the same word for 'brier' is found, but instead of its usual-ly accompanying word for 'thorns', here another word occurs, one that is also found in Isaiah 33.12 and in a number of other places in the Old Testament. Thus it has to be said that in the main list of references given above we do have a definite series of occurrencies of two 'Isaianic' words, two words that in the main occur together, and in what we have called the first part (chapters 1 to 39) of the book of Isaiah. These two words, and especially in their combination together, 'thorns and briers', paint a picture of a deep and dreadful devastation of the land, stressing its inhos-pitable nature as far as human beings are concerned, and as regards the will and purpose of the Lord its failure to produce any good and worthwhile growth. There are two further occur-rences of 'thorns' in the book of Isaiah, in 7.19 and 55.13, but a different Hebrew word is employed in these. In the first, the situ-ation as far as the land and its produce are concerned is entirely neutral, but in the second, which occurs in the final peroration of the thrilling oracles that make up chapters 40 to 55, we are given

an assuring and heart-warming picture of a land transformed by
the activity of the Lord, in which in place of thorns there will be
cypresses, instead of the brier (again a different word from that of
the earlier occurrences, and a word, in fact, that makes here its
one and only appearance in the whole of the Old Testament) will
come up the myrtle.

To return to the contrast in Isaiah 24 to 27 between the present sinful city and the future one in which there is peace and
justice, we may profitably consider the great theological work of
St Augustine, *The City of God*. This was written between AD 413
and 426 when Augustine was bishop of Hippo, but the impulse
that gave rise to it was the fall of Rome to Alaric in 410, an event
that caused deep consternation throughout the Roman world.
Augustine describes two different cities. In one place he says,

> This is assuredly the great difference that sunders the two
> cities of which we are speaking: the one is a community
> of devout men, the other a company of the irreligious,
> and each has its own angels attached to it. In one city love
> of God has been given first place, in the other, love of self.

And elsewhere Augustine has this to say:

> We see then that the two cities were created by two kinds
> of love: the earthly city was created by self-love reaching
> the point of contempt for God, the Heavenly City by the
> love of God carried as far as contempt of self. In fact, the
> earthly city glories in itself, the Heavenly City glories in
> the Lord ... The one city loves its own strengths shown in
> its powerful leaders; the other says to its God, 'I will love
> you, my Lord, my strength.' [31]

Even so, notwithstanding all that Augustine says, the most devoted and most passionate of religious believers may be forgiven
when they find it hard to believe that eventually the world and its
cities will be set free from what St Paul calls 'its bondage to decay'
(Romans 8.21), [32] and that it will really enter upon a new life of
joy and peace. Yet that was surely the belief held by those who in

their various ways were responsible for chapters 24 to 27 of the book of Isaiah. And believers who now turn to these oracles are surely intended to continue to hope in God and in his purposes. Here is hope for a creation that manifestly continues to be in bondage to corrupt powers. Indeed, it has been suggested that these four chapters of the Isaiah book were developed and formed so that eventually they, 'became a prayer-book for the eschatological groups, a handbook to strengthen their personal faith ... and a work of apologetic against their opponents'.[33]

What has been given to us in these chapters is something to strengthen the personal and corporate faith of believers today, and to encourage them in the face and challenge of those who have grown weary of waiting, and have either succumbed to evil, or become absorbed in the pursuit of wordly gain.

> It will be said on that day,
>> Lo, this is our God; we have waited for him,
>>> so that he might save us.
>> This is the Lord for whom we have waited;
>>> let us be glad and rejoice in his salvation.
> (Isaiah 25.9)

Chapters 28 to 32: Back to Judah and Jerusalem

Now it is Judah and Jerusalem again, but what we read in Isaiah 28 to 32 is no mere reprise of the contents of chapters 2 to 12. It is not a case of having been introduced to the context of Judah and Jerusalem's life and setting in the wider world of the nations in chapters 13 to 23, and having had Israelite history (and our own) set in the great and expansive time scale envisaged in chapters 24 to 27, that we now go back to Judah and Jerusalem on their own in the setting of a minor war of limited-time duration, the so-called Syro-Ephraimite war in chapters 7 and 8. Far from it. For it is clear that the contents of chapters 28 to 32 concern Judah and Jerusalem at a later historical moment than the one that predominates in chapters 2 to 12,[34] and further, the general political situation for Israelite people is now more grave than was the earlier one, in fact one that was becoming pregnant with fore-boding for the future.

When we last read about Judah and Jerusalem in the book of Isaiah, they were being attacked by that Syro-Ephraimite coalition, an event that was giving rise to a good deal of panic and consternation on the part of king and people (7.2). In this situation the prophet Isaiah counselled calm and trust in the Lord (7.7–9).

Now we can also read about this historical incident in 2 Kings 16.1–20 (and also for that matter in 2 Chronicles 28, though this does not need to concern us here[35]). In the account in the books of Kings we read that King Ahaz of Judah sent for help to Assyria, whose king at that time, as we have already seen, was Tiglath-pileser III, a leader who had assumed the Assyrian throne in 745 BC. This is what we are told:

> Ahaz sent messengers to King Tiglath-pileser of Assyria, saying, 'I am your servant and your son. Come up, and rescue me from the hand of the king of Aram [Syria] and from the hand of the king of Israel, who are attacking me.' (2 Kings 16.7)

Further, Ahaz sent a 'present', along with silver and gold from the Jerusalem temple and treasures from the royal palace, to the Assyrian king (v. 8), with the result that one way or another Ahaz received the desired help.

> The king of Assyria listened to him [Ahaz]; the king of Assyria marched up against Damascus [capital of Aram, Syria], and took it, carrying its people captive to Kir; then he killed Rezin [king of Aram, Syria]. (2 Kings 16.9)

We should perhaps not judge Ahaz too harshly for these actions, for it is reasonable to assume that he believed his country to be in real danger and that he as its king was acting responsibly in appealing to his powerful neighbour for help. When Ahaz spoke to Tiglath-pileser about being 'your servant and your son' (v. 7) he was in reality offering himself as a small vassal kingdom to the mighty power of Assyria. In fact, Ahaz was only doing what many a ruler of a small nation has done before and since, namely to form an alliance with a powerful neighbour to secure protection and peace for a geographically and politically small, and militarily weak, kingdom.

In no way at all was the relationship of Judah and Assyria one of equals. Far from it. Rather, by this arrangement Judah became a vassal state of the mighty Assyrian empire. And while on the positive side Judah gained the protection of the overlord and thus some sense of peace and security, on the negative side of the equation the cost lay in the taxation that was levied to pay for the benefit of the protection the overlord would give. This was at the loss of Judah's national freedom and independence. Two effects of all this would make themselves felt for many a long year for the people and their leaders of Judah and Jerusalem.

In the first place this meant that gone were the days when Israel and Judah were able to rule themselves, directing their own affairs of state. In fact, the northern kingdom of Israel had since 722 BC been in a state of vassalage to Assyria, and by the time of the kingship of Ahaz over Judah was in a more advanced state of subjection to the overlord than the one that Judah was then entering. This meant that the days of King David's empire were now long gone, those days when in various ways and by sundry alliances and arrangements there was an empire encompassing Judah, Jerusalem, Israel, Philistia, Moab, Aram, Edom and Ammon. What King David was able to pass on to his son and successor Solomon was of a totally different order and magnitude from what Ahaz some 250 or so years later was able to pass on to his son and successor, Hezekiah. Of course, by the yardstick of those later mighty empires of Assyria, Babylonia, Persia, Greece and Rome the total extent of David's old-time rule was small indeed. Yet in its own day it *had* been an empire, and in his day there *was* an element of greatness belonging to David as he ruled over his various nations from his city of Jerusalem. In those now far-off days Jerusalem was in a pre-eminent and predominant position among the capital cities in the empire. There was a real sense in which Israel and Judah did rule over a little world, and it must have been seen by some, or even many, that God was with his people, giving them his blessing and enabling them to gain victory over their enemies.

It does not take any great powers of imagination to appreciate than when in the reign of Ahaz in Jerusalem the small state of Judah had to accept vassalage to the Assyrians, that thereby some serious theological questions were raised for various people. Were not the people of Judah and Jerusalem the special possession of the Lord who was believed to be none other than the Lord God of Israel, and was not this Lord believed to be with his people? What now was happening, and where was God in all this? Or, to come at the matter from another angle, what did this mean as far as the city of Jerusalem was concerned? At least in some quarters the belief was held that Jerusalem was held in a special and providential way in the care of God. Such a belief, it has been argued, finds expression in some of the Old Testament psalms, in particular Psalms 46, 47 and 48. [36] What then had taken place in this new situation when the holy city of Jerusalem was reduced to being no more than just one of those cities in a subservient role to the might and rule of Assyria? Was indeed the blessing of God any longer with his people, and if perchance it was, then in what way?

Much of the book of Isaiah may be said to be taken up with these issues. This is to say that in a series of changing historical settings – all too often ones that appear to reflect a generally deteriorating social and political situation for people in Judah and Jerusalem, yet elsewhere apparently relating to times of new hope, new possibilities and something of a restoration of some earlier conditions – the concern in the book is to seek a theological interpretation of such events. What do these situations mean for God's people, what is happening, and why is it happening? Is God still the God of gods, and does he still have his almighty powers? Is Jerusalem still the chosen city of God? These are questions to which we shall be returning, and we shall be reflecting upon what there is in the book of Isaiah in response to changing national and international situations.

A second consequence of this subservient position in which Judah and Jerusalem (never mind Israel) found themselves, was a besetting temptation, whenever the time seemed ripe, to attempt rebellion against Assyria. In moments of Assyrian weakness, or in times when Assyrian rulers were preoccupied with other – possibly troublesome – parts of their empire, the temptation was always there to some group or other to suggest trying to break free from the yoke. An associated temptation going with this was to look to Egypt for help and support in such a venture. It seems that at such times there was usually in Jerusalem a group who would argue that salvation lay in the Egyptian direction, that sufficient and willing help was there available, and that now was the moment to make the bid for freedom from Assyria. Isaiah chapter 20, for example, is a polemic against trusting in the might of Egypt, while in the chapters now before us, Isaiah 28–32, we have words about, and in reaction to, attempts to rebel against the king of Assyria.

What we have then in chapters 28 to 32 is a series of sayings, the burden of some of these being condemnation of leaders and people, the theme of others being expressions of hope for days to come, the assurance of a good and blessed future under God. For example in 28.1–13 there are somewhat severe words against the political leaders of Ephraim, that is the old northern kingdom of Israel. Perhaps we have to understand these words as being addressed to the rump 'state' (a very much reduced state) left to Israel / Ephraim in the aftermath of the Syro-Ephraimite war in around 734 BC (see 2 Kings 17.1–6). Yet we should not think that either authorities or people in Jerusalem were escaping without criticism. Far from it, for they are lambasted in 28.14–22 and 29.9–16. In the first of these it is the political authorities that are under fire, being warned that the work of God in his coming in judgement upon them will indeed seem 'strange' and 'alien' (28.21). In the second it is prophets and people who are under condemnation:

> Because these people draw near with their mouths

> and honour me with their lips,
>   while their hearts are far from me,
> and their worship of me is a human commandment
>   learned by rote;
>   so I will again do
>   amazing things with this people,
>   shocking and amazing.
> The wisdom of their wise shall perish,
>   and the discernment of the discerning shall
>   be hidden. (Isaiah 29.13–14)

One particular manifestation of folly is now laid bare, and that is
the pursuit of alliances with Egypt. This is gross folly because it
is a seeking of help where in fact there is no help, seeking strength
where there is no strength (see 30.1–5, 6–7; 31.1–9). Yes,

> Alas for those who go down to Egypt for help
>   and who rely on horses,
> who trust in chariots because they are many
>   and in horsemen because they are very strong,
> but do not look to the Holy One of Israel
>   or consult the Lord! (Isaiah 31.1)

That is the issue: these people do not look to the Holy One of
Israel. Rather have they rejected the Lord's word given to them
through the medium of prophecy (30.8–14), and further have
rejected the real way of peace and life (30.15–17; 32.9–14). All
this has led to the holy city of Jerusalem being itself under attack
(29.1–4). Just as in those far off days when David laid siege to it
and conquered it (2 Sam. 5.6–10), so now it will be none other
than the Lord who himself besieges it.

> And like David I will encamp against you;
>   I will besiege you with towers
>   and raise siege-works against you. (Isaiah 29.3)

Yet there is to be a future, in the first place because the Lord's
anger will turn against Assyria for the way that that nation has

overstepped the mark in being used in God's purposes and has placed on the people 'a bridle that leads them astray' (30.27–33). In the second place there is to be a real change in fortunes for the people of Judah and Jerusalem. This is expressed in Isaiah 29.5–8, 17–24, in 30.18–26, and in 32.1–8. Nor to be forgotten is 32.15–20 which speaks of the wilderness becoming a fruitful field, another example of that re-use of image and metaphor in the book of Isaiah that we have observed earlier. Whereas 7.23–25 spoke of the fruitful land becoming a wilderness, here in 32.15–20 is the reversal, the wilderness becoming a fruitful field. And then (because here we are dealing with imagery and metaphor, so that while the words say one thing they are intended to signify something else) …

> Then justice will dwell in the wilderness,
>   and righteousness abide in the fruitful field.
> The effect of righteousness will be peace,
>   and the result of righteousness, quietness and
>   trust for ever.
> My people will abide in a peaceful habitation,
>   in secure dwellings, and in quiet resting-places.
> (Isaiah 32.16–18)

For above all this human activity, or lack of it, and beyond the human folly with just-occasional flashes of wisdom, there is still the Lord working out his purposes. In Isaiah 28 there is talk of the Lord's work and this is expressed through the imagery of a farmer who does different things at different seasons, and yet all is done at the appropriate time so that in the long term all will be done and all will be well. And here, once again, we have another example of the re-use in the Isaiah book of an image that was employed earlier. Here again is the thought of that barren land of 7.23–25, now transformed as it is spoken about in 32.15–20. There is also here something by way of looking back at the parable of the Lord and his vineyard in 5.1–7, where the owner (the Lord) takes such care over the preparation of the ground and with doing all that needs to be done for successful viticulture.

How can this be? This can be because the Lord will do it, as the great divine Farmer at work in his fields, working the appropriate works through the various seasons in the year. Thus,

> Do those who plough for sowing plough continually?
> Do they continually open and harrow their ground?
> When they have levelled its surface,
> do they not scatter dill, sow cummin,
> and plant wheat in rows
> and barley in its proper place,
> and spelt as the border? ...
>
> Grain is crushed for bread,
> but one does not thresh it for ever;
> one drives the cartwheel and horses over it,
> but one does not pulverize it.
> This also comes from the Lord of hosts;
> he is wonderful in counsel,
> and excellent in wisdom. (Isaiah 28.24–25, 28–29)

Chapters 33 to 39 : Towards the future – a triptych

In order to understand these chapters we need both to recall what precedes them and also observe what follows. The preceding material has already been considered, and it has been noted how it sets forth various prophetic reactions, some of them Isaiah's and some of them from other prophets, yet all of them concerning a people who for so much of the time acted in foolish ways, who for so much of the time were led in foolish ways, and who lived in the shadow, an ever-growing and continually darkening shadow, of the Assyrian empire. Certainly, in chapters 28 to 32 there is this real sense of the presence, even menace, of the might of Assyria.

Yet beyond chapters 33 to 39 is something totally different. From chapter 40 onwards there is material that displays a very different emphasis. There is talk about forgiveness and new life, about the glorious possibility of a return home, along with an associated call to prepare for the journey, a journey that will involve a trek through desert areas. In fact this journey will be something of a new 'exodus', the old one being the journey made from Egypt to Canaan under the leadership of Moses about which we read in the book of Exodus. As we shall come to see, Isaiah 40 to 55 does contain 'exodus' language, in the sense that some of the essential message of these chapters is expressed through the portrayal of a new exodus, that is, in a new age God's people are being rescued and led home in rather the same way that the ancestors of those people many centuries ago were rescued from Egypt and led to a new land and home.

But from where is this new exodus, and to where, and when? As we shall come to see, the most likely setting of Isaiah 40 to 55 is in the closing years of the Babylonian exile, an exile that for the people of Judah and Jerusalem began in 598 BC with the first deportation of people to Babylon by the Babylonians, who by that time had taken over from the Assyrians as the dominant power in Mesopotamia, and who in 587 BC totally overan Jerusalem, setting fire to the city and its temple complex, and deporting many more of its inhabitants. We read about these events in 2 Kings 24 to 25. Yet, as before and also ever since, 'kingdoms rise and wane' and the Babylonian empire came to its zenith and then waned. In particular, the Persian ruler Cyrus (the Great) entered Babylon in triumph in 539 BC and inaugurated a new era. It was certainly a new era for the subject peoples of the now-defeated Babylonian empire, for Cyrus allowed them to go home, to go back to their own lands and moreover to worship their own gods.

We shall return to these matters when we come to Isaiah 40 to 55, but this short and anticipatory excursus has been necessary so that we can begin to see the purpose and significance of the chapters in the book of Isaiah that follow on from 1 to 32, chapters that have a primary focus on Judah and Jerusalem in times prior to the deportations to Babylon, and that are followed by 40 to 55, chapters exuding a message of hope and joy, expressing supreme confidence that the Lord will effect their return to their homeland.

We can now focus on Isaiah 33 to 39, and we need to see them as providing something of a bridge between the preceding and following parts of the book. It is not that these chapters actually deal with the exile. They do not say how the exile occurred, nor do they give any details about the Babylonian (and elsewhere) life of those erstwhile inhabitants of Judah and Jerusalem – in fact they do not actually say that an exile took place. Yet they do bridge the gap where from a historical point of view the exile occurred, in particular seeking to interpret from a theological point of view why and how it is that a dominant theme of chapters 1 to 32 is the Lord's judgement upon his people for their sinfulness whereas the themes of 40 to 55 are divine forgiveness and the possibilities of new life and hope.

Chapters 33 to 39 fall into three readily distinquishable blocks, namely chapter 33, chapters 34 to 35, and chapters 36 to 39. My own suggestion is that together they form something of a triptych, that is a composition akin to those paintings that consist of three parts, panels or canvasses, and frequently adopted for altarpieces in the Medieval and Renaissance ages, hinged together at the sides, and usually through their three paintings portraying the same theme or else giving expression to different aspects of it. I suggest that we understand Isaiah 33, 34 to 35 and 36 to 39 in this manner, for each of these in its own particular way (and they are each of them quite different from the others) paints a picture in words, and such a picture that we are carried over in thought from the earlier chapters of the book to the later ones, from chapters 1 to 32 to chapters 40 to 66, and in particular to chapters 40 to 55. This process takes place in the following way.

First consider chapter 33. It has frequently been observed that this chapter appears to be something of a hotch-potch, a huggermugger of brief and varied short sections.[37] Many years ago Hermann Gunkel, a German Old Testament scholar (1862–1932), suggested that this chapter was to be understood as a prophetic liturgy, and I believe that this is the way it should be regarded. It is not so much that it was actually a prophetic liturgy: about that we do not know, certainly having no evidence that it was used in that way. Yet what we *may* say is that the chapter is *expressed* in the form of a liturgy, that it is presented *as if it were* a liturgy.[38] What we have in this chapter are contrasting pieces of material some of which are thoroughly down-to-earth, speaking of the reality of things present in the contemporary world, 'warts and all', alongside other parts that convey confident visions of peace and a life of well-being under the care of God. It is indeed a chapter of realities and visions, at times grim realities, at other times splendid visions.

Thus, for example, verses 7–9 are about grim realities.

> Listen! the valiant cry in the streets;
> the envoys of peace weep bitterly.
> The highways are deserted,
> travellers have left the road.
> The treaty is broken,
> its oaths are despised,
> its obligation is disregarded.
> The land mourns and languishes;
> Lebanon is confounded and withers away;
> Sharon is like a desert;
> and Bashan and Carmel shake off their leaves.
> (Isaiah 33.7–9)

But how different is the vision spoken about in verse 20:

> Look on Zion, the city of our appointed festivals!
> Your eyes will see Jerusalem,
> a quiet habitation, an immovable tent,
> whose stakes will never be pulled up,
> and none of whose ropes will be broken.
> (Isaiah 33.20)

Surely this belongs to the world of worship, where and in which worshippers are invited prayerfully and sorrowfully to contemplate the present realities of their lives, and where and in which also in a spirit of worship and faith in God they are to rise above this distress and to dream holy dreams of a new order of earthly things.

Can we not understand how appropriate is this medium of worship to express this confidence in God's purposes on earth, and to set forth such a vision? In worship the devotees of God both lament their present situations and distresses, and yet also in faith and hope enter into that other world of the divine, and see earthly things as they one day will surely be. Thus Isaiah 33, as the first picture of the triptych, carries its readers and hearers from the reality of the present (that is so much expressed in the various parts that make up chapters 1 to 32), and carries them over into the new world of hope expressed in chapters 40 to 66, especially in 40 to 55. And this, the first 'picture' of the triptych is expressed in the language of worship, in the form of a liturgy.

So to the second picture (chapters 34 and 35) of the triptych, and we shall have to spend somewhat longer on this than on the first (chapter 33). This picture is expressed in a very different style from that of the previous one. It is expressed in what is known as proto-apocalyptic language, a style of writing that we have already encountered in Isaiah 24 to 27. Isaiah 34 and 35 are generally regarded as belonging together. R. E. Clements regards them as a unity, but more commonly the differences in their togetherness have been emphasised, and thus the word 'diptych' (not to be confused with my triptych!) has sometimes been used of them.[39] In all probability these chapters come from the time after the exile, that is as far as Jerusalem is concerned in the Second Temple period. Certainly, in chapter 35 there are echoes of the language, imagery and confident outlook of chapters 40 to 55.[40]

In chapter 34 the nation of Edom is at the centre of things, but in an evil sense. This is the nation that epitomises hostility to the will and purpose of God, a role taken over from Babylon, which in turn had taken it over from Assyria. Thus what we have here are extremely strong words against Edom, and the threat of a cataclysmic end to this nation, so much so that 'the mountains shall flow with their blood' (v. 3) and 'their land shall be soaked with blood, and their soil made rich with fat' (v. 7). The result of this terrible destruction will be that the land will revert to being a wilderness, a theme that we have already encountered earlier in the book of Isaiah.[41]

No doubt this will appear butal, even barbaric, but we should perhaps realise that for Jewish people of post-exilic times Edom was the apotheosis of all those peoples who stood opposed to the will of God. The particular crime against Judah that put the Edomites in such odious contempt seems to have been their incursion into the land of Judah at the time of Judean weakness following the fall of Jerusalem in 587 BC. In the third main part of the book of Isaiah there is a passage that portrays a dreadful execution of the judgement of the Lord upon perfidious Edom (Isaiah 63.1–3), a passage that we are surely intended to understand as an expression of confidence in the ultimate triumph of the purposes of God.[42]

The final two verses of this chapter (34.16–17) take up once again the imagery of a written document. At certain points of the book of Isaiah we have references to details being recorded in a written document (8.16; 30.8).[43] In Isaiah 8.16 and 30.8 it is the prophet's word that is to be recorded in writing, a word of the Lord to his people through his prophet but a word to which unfortunately those people have been deaf. But here in 34.16 the written piece is given the title 'the book of the Lord', and we should perhaps understand this as referring to a document recording some of the words of a prophet, or of a number of prophets, that may well in the fulness of time have come to be incorporated into the book of Isaiah that we have and know. This is also significant in that here there is a real sense of the elevation given to the status of the word of the prophet in that it has come to be incorporated into 'the book of the Lord'. However, as to the date of this document, or anything about its extent, we have no information and must admit our ignorance.[44] What, however, we should note is that this talk about 'the book of the Lord' serves to invest an increased sense of importance, even authority, in the prophet's words here recorded. That is to say, the doom of Edom (for which we are intended to understand 'all the enemies of the Lord') is sealed – 'his doom is writ'.

Therefore let the faithful be assured, and at the same time let the sinners be warned!

Then there is the second part of chapters 34 to 35, the second picture of the diptych, chapter 35, one of the most thrilling chapters in the whole of the Old Testament. This speaks first of a transformation of the world of nature, a further occurrence of a theme we have already had cause to take notice of a number of times. See above on Isaiah 27.4. In the present context we read about a confidently-expected blossoming in the world of nature that stands in marked contrast with the talk of the wilderness in chapter 34. Thus instead of thorns, nettles and thistles (34.13) in the future there will be reeds and rushes (35.7), instead of polluted waters (34.9) there will be waters in the wilderness, streams in the desert (35.6), what used to be a safe environment for the jackals (34.13) will become a swamp (35.7), where travel was well-nigh impossible (34.10) now there will be a highway, indeed a 'holy way' (35.8), and so on. Thus, those who feel discouraged about the general situation around them are to take heart and be encouraged, for the reason that the Lord is coming, coming to exact retribution upon those who are opposed to him (35.3–4). Above all there is the word to the faithful, 'He will come and save you.' (35.4)

This will make possible the transformation not only of nature but also of people. Thus the blind will see, the deaf will hear, the disabled leap, the dumb shout (35.5–6). And as for that transformed wilderness, it will become the 'holy way' (v. 8) which, unattended by dangers from wild animals, will become fit for the 'redeemed' (v. 9), the 'ransomed of the Lord' to travel on and thus come to Zion with joy (mentioned twice) and gladness, for 'sorrow and sighing shall flee away' (v. 10).

Now the language of 35.5–10 is permeated with the images, pictures, metaphors and similes that, as we shall come to see, are found in such abundance in Isaiah 40 to 55.[45] Thus the blind will see (35.5; 42.7, 16), waters will burst out in the desert (35.6–7; 41.17–18; 43.20), the burning sands will become a pool (35.7; 41.18–19), and there will be the highway (35.8; 40.3–5) upon which the exiles now returning home may come to Zion (35.10; 51.11). But whereas, as we shall come to see, chapters 40 to 55 are given a definite linkage into a particular historical setting, through reference to Cyrus the Persian ruler having been called by God (44.24—45.7), chapter 35 is in contrast generalised, no historical setting being mentioned. Thus chapter 35 is imaginative, thrilling and hopeful, and its confident forward-looking spirit is all of a piece with that of chapters 40 to 55. Whether chapter 35 comes from the author of 40 to 55, or whether rather it is a composition of another person in the style and language of 40 to 55, cannot any longer be determined.

What however is clear is that, along with chapter 33, the diptych in chapters 34 to 35 serves to carry us over from the earlier pre-exilic setting, spoken about in parts of chapters 1 to 32, into the new setting of the time after the exile. Further, this unit of chapters 34 and 35 does this through the combination of a chapter expressed in proto-apocalyptic language (34) with the other in the thrilling language of chapters 40 to 55 (35). Thus in their present distresses and confusions let the hands of God's faithful people be strengthened and their feeble knees be made firm (35.3) – and also, let the reader of the completed book of Isaiah be made aware that in age after age the purposes of God go on!

> Say to those who are of a fearful heart,
>   'Be strong, and do not fear!
> Here is your God.
>   He will come with vengeance,
> with terrible recompense.
>   He will come and save you.' (Isaiah 35.4)

The third picture of the group of three pictures – what I have called a triptych – is in Isaiah 36 to 39 and is written in a different style, and uses different vocabulary, from either of the two preceding pictures.[46] Much of this is in prose rather than poetry, and reads very much like parts of the books of Kings. In fact, large parts of Isaiah 36 to 39 are actually to be found in 2 Kings, though with some differences. It is generally considered that the material here that is in both Kings and Isaiah had an earlier use in Kings and at a later stage was incorporated into Isaiah. [47] Yet it was not taken over just as it was, but some alterations were made, alterations that at first sight may appear small and trifling, but which on closer examination are seen to be significant. We shall consider these three 'alterations', each in the context of the particular section of these chapters where it is found. [48]

The first unit of material in Isaiah 36 to 39 is the story of the dreadful siege of Jerusalem in 701 BC by Sennacherib king of Assyria who ruled from about 705 to 681 BC. We read about this in 2 Kings 18.13—19.37 and in Isaiah 36.1—37.38, but the Isaiah version is shorter than the Kings. The shortening occurs at the beginning, where 2 Kings 18.13–16 is reduced to just one verse in Isaiah.

> In the fourteenth year of King Hezekiah, King Sennacherib of Assyria came up against all the fortified cities of Judah and captured them. (Isaiah 36.1)

Now what has been omitted here in the carrying over of this material from what there is in the books of Kings? It is 2 Kings 18.14–16, three verses that speak of Hezekiah confessing to Sennacherib that he has done wrong, that tell of gifts of temple treasures that he gave to the Assyrian king. It is as if the Kings account has been 'doctored' as it has gone into Isaiah in order to give a better picture of, impression of Hezekiah. The Judean king here in the Isaiah account does not fly into a panic on having his great city besieged, nor does he try to buy Jerusalem off its peril. Hezekiah comes over to us in the Isaiah account as calm and collected, trusting in God. And no doubt that is what the editors of the Isaiah version want us to believe.

We come to the next 'alterations' when we read about an illness that King Hezekiah had. This is in Isaiah 38.1–22, which is paralleled by 2 Kings 20.1–11. The talk of the siege of Jerusalem is still there, but to this has been added the further calamity that the king has been afflicted with a boil, and become seriously ill. In fact the prophet Isaiah suggested that Hezekiah should prepare for the worst (2 Kings 20.1; Isaiah 38.1), but as a result of prayer (2 Kings 20.2–3; Isaiah 38.2–3), and of the application of a fig poultice (2 Kings 20.7; Isaiah 38.21), the king recovered. To what extent the recovery was due on the one hand to prayer and on the other to the poultice we, of course, do not know, and nor is any opinion vouchsafed in these accounts. However, what is our present and particular interest in the two accounts of this incident is the fact that no less than *two* changes have been made to the material as it was brought over into the Isaiah book.

The first of these occurs between 2 Kings 20.6b and Isaiah 38.6, and is as follows. In 2 Kings 20.6b we read (it is the Lord who is speaking),

> I will deliver you and this city out of the hand of the king of Assyria; I will defend this city for my own sake and for my servant David's sake.

Whereas in Isaiah 38.6 we have only,

> I will deliver you and this city out of the hand of the king of Assyria, and I will defend this city.

That is, there is no mention in the Isaiah account of the Lord defending the city for his own sake, or the sake of the king of the line of David. Here, the Lord's resolve is to defend the city 'full stop'. Such is his will and purpose, and this is not for any rather more particular reason of saving the reputation of himself or his earthly king. Rather, here is an unambiguous and reassuring message of the Lord's protection for Hezekiah ('you', singular) and Jerusalem ('this city') – and thus for all the city's people.

The second of these changes in this passage that speaks of Hezekiah's nasty boil is different from the first insomuch as this time there is additional material in the Isaiah account as compared with that in Kings. The extra piece that we have in Isaiah is Isaiah 38.9–20, and is in the form of what we call a lament, that is, a deep and heartfelt prayer uttered to God from the depths of a person's agony. We know these laments in other parts of the Old Testament, especially in the book of Psalms, and we frequently observe in them a quite startling change of mood at the end in which the person praying moves from a sense of despair to one of profound trust in God for the future. [49] Here, the lament is not present in the Kings account, but it makes its appearance in the Isaiah account and at the end has Hezekiah, portrayed as a deeply pious king giving praise to God for his deliverance, ending his lament on a note of real confidence.

> The Lord will save me,
>> and we will sing to stringed instruments
> all the days of our lives,
>> at the house of the Lord. (Isaiah 38.20)

Now, taking stock of these changes made as the Kings material was adapted for use in Isaiah we observe that there is a definite emphasis upon the theme of 'deliverance', the deliverance that God gives to his city, his people in their distresses, and to their king in his particular danger and distress. We see this in the calm trust that Hezekiah displays as his city is attacked by the Assyrian army with Sennacherib at its head (Isaiah 36.1), in the promise of the Lord that he will defend and deliver his city in a general way and sense (Isaiah 38.6), and in the way that Hezekiah is portrayed as making his statement about the delivering power of the Lord, a generalising statement that is portrayed as proceeding from the thankful King Hezekiah having been granted deliverance from his troublesome boil (Isaiah 38.20).

And – as if to make the point absolutely clear, or at least to make sure that the reader or the hearer of these chapters has fully grasped this theme of the delivering will and power of God – there is one further change to be noted as the Kings material was adapted for its new setting in the Isaiah work. This is in the third of the three incidents that we read about in Isaiah 36 to 39, the first being the siege of Jerusalem (2 Kings 18.13—19.37; Isaiah 36.1—37.38) and the second King Hezekiah's illness (2 Kings 20.1–11; Isaiah 38.1–22). The third concerns the visit of the envoys of Merodach Baladan (the son of Baladan, the king of Babylon) to Hezekiah in Jerusalem (2 Kings 20.12–19; Isaiah 39.1–8). Here there is a significant change in wording to be noted between these accounts. Hezekiah has shown these envoys all his treasures, and the prophet Isaiah has given him a somewhat stinging rebuke, warning him that the end result of his actions could be exile in Babylon for Hezekiah himself and his people (2 Kings 20.16–18; Isaiah 39.5–7). What does the king say to his prophet in response? In the account in Kings that response is couched in the form of a question, which reads, literally,

> And Hezekiah said to Isaiah, 'Good is the word of the
> Lord which you have spoken'. And he said, 'Is it not if it
> is peace and security in my days?' (2 Kings 20.19)

But in Isaiah there is no question. What in Kings was a question has become in Isaiah a statement, a plain statement of fact. Again literally, it reads,

> And Hezekiah said to Isaiah, 'Good is the word of the
> Lord which you have spoken'. And he said, 'For it will be
> peace and security in my days'. (Isaiah 39.8)

And that is what these chapters 36 to 39 in Isaiah are about, namely, the message of deliverance, peace and security. Yet at the same time they do not hide the fact that there are difficult times ahead. The theme of exile has been aired, its damoclean sword has been hung over Hezekiah by Isaiah as the prophet has exposed the king's folly and naivety in showing the Babylonian envoys all those Jerusalem treasures. Now the Babylonians know what resources and armaments there are in Jerusalem; all has been revealed!

> Then Isaiah said to Hezekiah, 'Hear the word of the
> Lord of hosts: Days are coming when all that is in your
> house, and that which your ancestors have stored up until
> this day, shall be carried to Babylon; nothing shall be left,
> says the Lord. Some of your own sons who are born to
> you shall be taken away; they shall be eunuchs in the
> palace of the king of Babylon.' (Isaiah 39.5–7)

Thus here in Isaiah 36 to 39 is the message about the coming exile, and yet also the assurance that with the Lord there will be deliverance, peace and security. Indeed, if we may speak in the most general terms concerning the overall themes and progression of thought in the book of Isaiah, we may perhaps say that there is within chapters 1 to 32 that distinct motif of the judgement of the Lord upon his people, yet that talk of deliverance, peace and security will come very much to the fore in Isaiah 40 and the chapters that follow.

And this is where what I have called the triptych, those three pictures in Isaiah 33 to 39, comes in. The triptych is intended to serve as three ways of expressing the fact that while under God there may be judgement, yet also will there be be mercy and security. They are intended to make a bridge between those difficult situations spoken about in the earlier part of the book and those much more hopeful parts that will follow. That is, while we are intended from our reading of chapters 1 to 32 to become convicted about the reality and seriousness of sin and evil, and about the associated judgement of the holy God upon them, yet at the same time we are not intended to go away with the idea that that is the last word of God, or in any way that his judgement will be his last act. Far from it! Rather, as we shall very soon see, a prophet will be called to proclaim 'comfort' to his people (Isaiah 40.1), and to assure them that they are not forgotten by their God. But in order that the transition be made from the earlier to the later parts of the book, we have been given these three pictures, the first (chapter 33) expressed in the language of worship, the second (chapters 34 to 35) in assuring and reassuring words about coming days of change for the better for God's people, and the third (chapters 36 to 39) in the form of stories that clearly have been adopted and adapted so as to speak of the ongoing reality of God's deliverance of his people and of his associated gift to them of peace and security.

And thus does the first part of the book of Isaiah come to its close.

II

CHAPTERS 40 TO 55

Isaiah chapter 40 begins not only abruptly but also thrillingly. It begins abruptly in that suddenly and without any announcement or preparation we are made aware that we are reading about a new and different situation. A whole new matter is being spoken about, and the language used to describe this situation is different from what has been encountered earlier in the book. Then, as well as this sense of abruptness, there is a thrilling note in what is being spoken about. No longer are there threats and denunciations, no longer are there warnings of coming exile, but here is talk of the forgiveness of past sins and the call to go out and make a new start in life. The chapter opens with a command from God to a group that is not named. The command is in the plural, that is, more than one person is being addressed. Thus,

> Comfort, O Comfort my people,
>   says your God.
> Speak tenderly to Jerusalem,
>   and cry to her
> that she has served her term,
>   that her penalty is paid,
> that she has received from the Lord's hand
>   double for all her sins. (Isaiah 40.1–2)

It would appear that here a group of prophets is receiving a divine call to a ministry of 'comforting', a ministry of assurance that a great and good new future lies before 'Jerusalem', that is 'the people of Jerusalem'. It becomes clear as one reads on in this chapter and the subsequent ones that those who are being addressed are the Israelite people, who in these chapters are frequently called Jacob (as in 40.27), or, as here in 40.2, Jerusalem, those people whose city, it will emerge, is at present in ruins (as in 52.9).

It does seem that the setting for all this is Babylon, in particular the closing years of the exile of Israelite people there. These are the people of Judah and Jerusalem who in 598 and 587 BC were forcibly deported to Babylon, about whom we read in 2 Kings 24 and 25, and about whose future we had been warned in Isaiah 39.5–7. Certainly the setting for Isaiah 40 to 55 would appear to be Babylon: [50] we hear much about Babylonian gods, in particular reading in these chapters a series of tirades against them to the effect that they are fairly useless gods, paper-tiger gods (44.9–20; 46.1–2), and that the God of the real power is the Lord God of Israel (40.12–31; 46.3–13). Yet that point surely needed to be made, for in the events of defeat for the people of Israel, and their city – and also apparently, their God – in 598 and 587 BC, and in the intervening years of exile in Babylon, it must have seemed that it was the gods of Babylon who were the really powerful, triumphant deities, far more so than the Lord God of Israel. Why, the city of Jerusalem was levelled to a heap and the holy temple was burnt with fire, and the armies of Babylon were experiencing the rich fruits of military victory (2 Kings 25.8–21)! Surely it must have looked as if the Lord God of Israel was something of a beaten God.

Not so, is the message of these thrilling chapters, Isaiah 40 to 55. Here is the assurance that in spite of any possible worldly evidences to the contrary the Lord God reigns (52.7), and is indeed the incomparable God. This is confidently set forth right at the beginning of these chapters, Isaiah 40.12–26 being a sustained paean of praise of the incomparable Holy One (v. 25). He has created all things, he knows all his creation, and – above all, and in spite of any possible evidences that may suggest otherwise – he knows his own people and certainly has not forgotten them (40.27–31). While those people may grow weary, he never will, and those who look to him will find in him ever new, fresh and abundantly adequate reserves of strength and energy.

Moreover, this Lord is to secure his people's release from their exile in Babylon and bring them back to their homeland. This he will do with power and might, making all due provision for them on their perilous journey.

> Thus says the Lord,
>   your Redeemer, the Holy One of Israel:
> For your sake I will send to Babylon
>   and break down all the bars,
>   and the shouting of the Chaldeans will be turned
>   to lamentation.
> I am the Lord, your Holy One,
>   the Creator of Israel, your King.
> Thus says the Lord,
>   who makes a way in the sea,
>   a path in the mighty waters,
> who brings out chariot and horse,
>   army and warrior;
> they lie down, they cannot rise,
>   they are extinquished, quenched like a wick:
> Do not remember the former things,
>   or consider the things of old.
> I am about to do a new thing;
>   now it springs forth, do you not perceive it?
> I will make a way in the wilderness
>   and rivers in the desert. (Isaiah 43.14–19)

How can this be? How will it be effected? According to the prophet of these chapters this will take place because the Lord is using the Persian ruler Cyrus as the human agent in his divine plans. Cyrus had seized power in the Median kingdom, and in 539 BC had entered Babylon in triumph. He took steps to secure the protection of the Babylonian temples and at the same time he allowed the Jewish subject people both to worship their own God and also to return to their own land. This Cyrus, says our prophet, has been taken and used to fulfil the will of the Lord:

> Who says of Cyrus, 'He is my shepherd,
>> and he shall carry out all my purpose';
> and who says of Jerusalem, 'It shall be rebuilt',
>> and of the temple, 'Your foundation shall be laid.'
> Thus says the Lord to his anointed, to Cyrus,
>> whose right hand I have grasped
> to subdue nations before him
>> and to strip kings of their robes,
> to open doors before him –
>> and the gates shall not be closed …
> (Isaiah 44.28—45.1)

In fact a great change of fortunes for the Babylonians and for the Jewish exiles is about to be experienced by both alike. The Babylonians who had been used to conditions of prosperity and the good things of life have very different ways coming upon them.

> Come down and sit in the dust,
>> virgin daughter Babylon!
> Sit on the ground without a throne,
>> daughter Chaldea!
> For you shall no more be called
>> tender and delicate.
> Take the millstones and grind meal,
>> remove your veil,
> strip off your robe, uncover your legs,
>> pass through the rivers.
> Your nakedness shall be uncovered,
>> and your shame shall be seen.
> I will take vengeance,
>> and I will spare no one.
> Our Redeemer – the Lord of Hosts is his name –
>> is the Holy One of Israel. (Isaiah 47.1–4)

Meanwhile the people of Israel are to pay attention to their God – the Lord of Hosts, the Holy One of Israel, as Isaiah 47.4 makes clear, using titles that we have already come across in the book of

Isaiah – who is in fact the first and the last (an expression that most likely means totality, that is, he is everything and he is everywhere and he is all things), the creator of the world and the Lord of the heavens.

> Listen to me, O Jacob,
>   and Israel, whom I called:
> I am He; I am the first,
>   and I am the last.
> My hand laid the foundation of the earth,
>   and my right hand spread out the heavens;
> when I summon them,
>   they stand at attention. (Isaiah 48.12–13)

These people are to prepare for departure from Babylon, a departure that will be infused with the note of joy that 'The Lord has redeemed his servant Jacob!' (48.20), and in the assurance that the inhospitable nature of the desert will be miraculously changed so that travel through it, and life in it, are made possible, rather in the same way that in the centuries-ago exodus from Egypt water was provided in the desert for the Israelite pilgrims. Thus,

> Go out from Babylon, flee from Chaldea,
>   declare this with a shout of joy, proclaim it,
> send it forth to the end of the earth;
>   say, 'The Lord has redeemed his servant Jacob!'
> They did not thirst when he led them through
>   the deserts;
>   he made water flow for them from the rock;
>   he split open the rock and the water gushed out.
> (Isaiah 48.20–21)

At this point we need to pause and say something about the prophet of these chapters, and about the manner and style in which his prophecies are expressed. We have already seen that there are two basic approaches to the issue of the authorship of Isaiah 40 to 55, namely that which understands that these chapters came from Isaiah of Jerusalem, these oracles and sayings, and all their associated background, having been seen in vision and recorded many years before their related events actually took place. The alternative view, and this is the view espoused in this present work, and also in my commentary on these chapters,[51] is that here we have a different author, one who lived in later times than that of the eighth-century prophet, Isaiah of Jerusalem, specifically that he lived in the closing years of the exile of Israelite people in Babylon. However, nowhere are we given the name of this author. Yet, as has already been observed, there are themes and vocabulary, concepts and expressions to be found right across the various parts of the whole book. This suggests to us that the later prophets worked in ways that would continue along the main lines and concerns, in accordance with the basic theological position, of the earlier, and yet at the same time in ways that would be appropriate for later times and all the associated new situations, concerns and conditions that went with those later ages. Perhaps it is only in 40.6, in the first person singular references, that the veil is just slightly lifted, revealing something of the calling of this prophet.[52]

As to the style of writing in these chapters, all are agreed as to its greatness and glory. It gives the impression that here is material for proclamation, preaching. If this be not preached material, then it is written in the style of oral proclamation. Frequently critics use the word 'rhetorical' to describe it, as does for example, Luis Alonso Schökel, who says that this prophet

> … ranks among the great religious poets. He is the poet of the return, the poet of hope. At first reading, we are struck by the rhetorical flow of the words: the broad, four-part parallelisms with a corresponding richness of vocabulary. It is a rhetoric directed to and against the audience, based on an enthusiastic and contagious lyricism. For the attentive ear, there is an exquisite sonorous quality which at moments reaches true virtuosity. Beyond this, there is a richness of imagery and a greatness of vision – greatness, not grandiosity. The poetry exhibits a freedom and joy

sufficient to close distances, boldness that reaches to the sky. All of this is joined by a passion that touches the heart and succeeds.[53]

Within these very distinctive chapters we find a number of distinctive modes of expression which can be mentioned only briefly here.[54] We have the Lord's announcing salvation (e.g. 41.17–20), or promising salvation (e.g. 41.8–13, 14–16). There are trial scenes where the Lord is imagined as a plaintiff, having a complaint against his people (e.g. 41.1–5, 21–29), and there are what have been called 'disputations' where it is the prophet, rather than the Lord, who is in dispute with his people (e.g. 40.12–17, 18–26, 27–31). And every now and again this prophet breaks into a hymn of praise (e.g. 42.10–13; 44.23; 49.13; 52.9–10), in expressions that are reminiscent of hymns of praise in the book of Psalms (e.g. Psalms 8; 29; 33; 46 to 48).

Chapters 40 to 48 address the Jewish exiles in Babylon, speaking to them about their God, their incomparable God, concerning his ongoing care for them, of his intention that they shall be involved in his ongoing purposes, and that they are destined to go home to Jerusalem. Let them do their part in preparing themselves for this journey, for other preparations are in train as a result of divine action, namely their way will be prepared, made smooth for them. Thus there will be something of a new exodus taking place; once again God's people will be led out of their land of captivity and be brought to a new land.[55]

Yet there is another theme that makes itself heard in these chapters, the theme of universalism. This is not an original theme as far as the Old Testament is concerned. The book of Amos opens with the prophet of that name surveying the nations around pre-exilic Israel and Judah, and proclaiming to the peoples of those various nations their sins and wrongdoings (Amos 1.3—2.3). As we have seen, the book of Isaiah also has a collection of oracles against the nations (Isaiah 13 to 23), and this 'international' thought is present in Isaiah 40 to 55 in a number of ways. In the first place there is an Israelite prophet apparently proclaiming the word of the Lord while, so it appears, he is in a foreign land, namely Babylon. The prophet's proclamation is that even there the Lord God of Israel is at work, certainly that his writ and authority are to be experienced there and responded to. At the same time the prophet proclaims that the gods of the Babylonians are powerless, and therefore useless, needing to be carried about the place on carts. Meanwhile, and in marked contrast, the Lord God carries his people all their days. The implication of this is that God's people are to understand that their God is there to carry them both in, and also from, their Babylonian land of exile.

In the second place the international theme in Isaiah 40 to 55 is to be observed in the various references to the fact that what the Lord God is going to do in the rescue of his people from Babylon is to be witnessed by a wide range of peoples and nations. Thus we encounter that recurring theme 'and all flesh shall see it together' (40.5; 41.20; 43.9; 49.26). That is, what the Lord is going to do for his people is portrayed as being something of an international spectacle.

Third, the international theme in Isaiah 40 to 55 appears in 42.1–4, the first of the four passages in these chapters which came to be grouped together by the scholar Bernhard Duhm (1847–1928) and which he called 'Servant Songs' (*Ebed-Lieder*). At this point we need to give some consideration to these four passages (Isaiah 42.1–4; 49.1–6; 50.4–9; 52.13—53.12). These are not really 'songs', rather passages about servanthood, perhaps we should say 'servant poems'. Further, they have come to be referred to as speaking of 'the suffering servant'. However, there is nothing in the first two of them (42.1–4; 49.1–6) about suffering, though to be sure there is much about suffering in the third and fourth (50.4–9; 52.13—53.12), and especially in the last in which we read of the servant's death and of his being raised to a new life. Then there is the question of the identity of the servant, or servants. Did the prophet have some individual in his mind when he wrote these passages?

The search for the identity of the servant has been long, complicated and involved. It may be remembered that Philip the

Evangelist in the Acts of the Apostles was asked by the Ethiopian travelling in his carriage and reading his Isaiah, in particular the fourth of the servant passages (52.13—53.12), 'About whom, may I ask you, does the prophet say this, about himself or about someone else?' (Acts 8.34). And it is as if in age after age, and particularly in the Christian Church, that question has gone on being asked, and that Old Testament scholars have propounded their theories and offered their varied and multifarious answers. Further, it has been in large measure as the Ethiopian framed his question that the debate has taken its course between the servant being understood either as the prophet himself (the so-called autobiographical theory), or else as some other individual. [56] The autobiographical theory has had something of a new lease of life in recent years, being set forth in two works by the late R. N. Whybray. [57] But in order to make this theory work Whybray had to suggest that in the fourth passage the servant did not actually die, but rather was in a 'deathly' situation, that he was near-to-death, almost 'as good as dead'. [58] Far more prevalent have been those theories propounding that the servant was an individual historical figure – and many have been the individuals suggested, from kings Hezekiah, Uzziah, Jehoiachin, and prophets Jeremiah and Ezekiel, to Moses, Cyrus (the Persian), or an unknown Rabbi who had leprosy. And, of course, there is another individual servant identity possibility that has featured over the years amongst these various theories, namely that he was the Messiah, understood by some scholars as the Messiah of Israel, and by Christian extrapolation as Jesus Christ, their Messiah. Meanwhile another group of theories has suggested that 'the servant' stands for a wider group, or even the whole people of Israel, or maybe a small part of the nation, the part that remains faithful, a remnant.

However, the approach taken here [59] is that we should not try to find one single servant that will fit what is said in all four passages. [60] My own view is that in these passages we are being given four pictures about how life will be for the people of God in coming days. I suggest that the prophet is saying that the days following the exile will be very different from pre-exilic times

when for a good while Israel and Judah were free, or at least reasonably free, to order their own lives and direct their national
affairs. Certainly in the heady days of kings David and Solomon
there was freedom for the nation to order its own life, and even
to dominate others, either militarily (David) or commercially
(Solomon). But exile changed all that, and showed, moreover, to
those who had eyes to see that the little Israelite nation if it ever
was to have an ongoing existence would not have one that had
any sense of a dominant or dominating role in the world of the
nations. Its Lord would not be revealed any more in never-failing
victories for them, his people, nor would those people be shown
to be his people by their unfailing victories over other nations.
Rather, those people of God would have to discover their life
under God in the role of servanthood, and they would have to
engage in a mission to the nations. Nor would this new people of
Israel be greater than the people of other nations, but rather they
would have to spend and be spent for others. This, I submit, is the
radical, revolutionary vision that is presented to us in the passages
in Isaiah 40 to 55 about the servant. [61]

The above has been a somewhat lengthy digression to deal with
the 'servant' passages, and it came out of the mention of the third
strand of 'internationalism' in Isaiah 40 to 55. The fact is that in
the first two servant passages the servant is entrusted with a mission to a wider world than that merely of the people of Israel.
Thus,

> Here is my servant, whom I uphold,
>   my chosen, in whom my soul delights;
> I have put my spirit upon him;
>   he will bring forth justice to the nations....
> He will not grow faint or be crushed
>   until he has established justice in the earth;
>   and the coastlands wait for his teaching.
> (Isaiah 42.1 and 4)

And,

he [the Lord] says,
'It is too light a thing that you should be my servant
    to raise up the tribes of Jacob
    and to restore the survivors of Israel;
I will give you as a light to the nations,
    that my salvation may reach to the end of the earth.'
(Isaiah 49.6)

Yet there is quite definitely talk of suffering in the third and fourth passages about the servant (Isaiah 50.4–9; 52.13—53.12), but this brings us into the second half of Isaiah 40 to 55, so we need to pause and remind ourselves where we have got to in that regard. While chapters 40 to 48 are very much dominated by the scene in Babylon, and have a good deal to say about the Babylonian gods, about Cyrus, about the 'former things',[62] now from chapter 49 onwards there is a new and different setting, that of Jerusalem. Here is the promise that the city will be rebuilt, in beauty and in much grandeur, and it will receive the exiles who return not only from Babylon but also from elsewhere. There is still the overall theme and conviction that the return from exile will take place, being made possible by the worldwide and almighty power, and set purpose, of the Lord (49.8–23; 50.1–3). Yet it is as if chapters 40 to 48 speak of the announcement and the beginning of the process, about the preparations in body, mind and spirit that the people must make, while chapters 49 to 55 are about the destination and completion of the journey.

In these chapters (49 to 55) the reality of the ruined city of Jerusalem is accepted, but with the assurance that its ruined walls are inscribed on the palms of the Lord's hands (49.16), but the place is to change, radically. The city is to,

Awake, awake,
    put on your strength, O Zion!
Put on your beautiful garments,
    O Jerusalem, the holy city;
for the uncircumcised and the unclean

> shall enter you no more.
> Shake yourself from the dust, rise up,
>   O captive Jerusalem;
> loose the bonds from your neck,
>   O captive daughter Zion! (Isaiah 52.1–2)

The city is bidden to listen to the messengers who bring it good news, the good news that the Lord has comforted his people and is redeeming Jerusalem (52.7–9). Indeed, the Lord is portrayed as rolling up his sleeves for this strenuous activity on behalf of his city and people, such strenuous activity that will be a worthy spectacle for the eyes of 'all the nations'.

> The Lord has bared his holy arm
>   before the eyes of all the nations;
> and all the ends of the earth shall see
>   the salvation of our God. (Isaiah 52.10)

Thus are the exiles to prepare themselves to leave Babylon and make the journey to Jerusalem. And not only must they prepare themselves for the journey through the desert area (in which, as with the first exodus, the Lord will make gracious and appropriate provision: 49.9–11), but they must also prepare themselves for what is a religious pilgrimage. They must purify themselves and be ready to carry the 'vessels of the Lord' (52.11), what must have been the old temple vessels used in the services and ceremonies in the pre-exilic Jerusalem temple. On its destruction by the Babylonians these vessels were removed by Nebuchadnezzar (2 Kings 25.14–15), and, according to Ezra 1.7–11 and 5.14–15, had been kept safe in Babylon. Now is the time for them to be taken to Jerusalem where, presumably, it is intended they will be used in the renewed worship of God in that place.[63] The pilgrimage will be, as before, in the presence and under the leadership of the Lord (Isaiah 52.12; compare Exodus 13.21; 14.19), but in contradistinction with the earlier exodus not in haste or flight (Isaiah 52.12; compare Exodus 12.11; Deuteronomy 16.3), or in danger of the enemy (Isaiah 52.12; Exodus 14.5–31).

Yet, triumphant and hopeful as these chapters are, there is that sombre note sounded in them that we cannot ignore. They are punctuated by the passages about the servant; in fact, no less than three of these occur in Isaiah 49 to 55 (49.1–6; 50.4–9; 52.13—53.12). We have already considered the first of these (49.1-6) and have noted that it concerns, as does 42.1-4, the call of a servant to a mission beyond the people of Israel. Here it is stated explicitly that the servant is Israel.

> And he [the Lord] said to me, 'You are my servant,
>> Israel, in whom I will be glorified.' (Isaiah 49.3)

For his part, the servant is more than conscious of failure in his calling, yet has continued to commit his cause to the Lord (v. 4). And then comes the surprise: this servant – in fact, Israel – is to be given a larger task, a mission to a wider world.

> I will give you as a light to the nations,
>> that my salvation may reach to the end of the earth.
> (Isaiah 49.6)

Still there is no mention of suffering – that is, until we come to the next servant passage (Isaiah 50.4–9), and here the talk is not so much about what the servant must do as he fulfils his mission, but is rather about his faithfulness and obedience to God.

> Morning by morning he wakens –
>> wakens my ear
>> to listen as those who are taught.
> The Lord God has opened my ear,
>> and I was not rebellious,
>> I did not turn backwards.
> (Isaiah 50.4b–5)

More, the servant did not resist the blows and insults he received from others as he was obedient to the divine word.

> I gave my back to those who struck me,
>> and my cheeks to those who pulled out the beard;

> I did not hide my face
> from insult and spitting. (Isaiah 50.6)

We are not given here specific details about the servant's ministry; perhaps it was one of sustaining and encouraging those who were weary, but whatever it was the servant did it with exemplary faithfulness as 'morning by morning' (v. 4) he is called back to the task, knowing that it is in his experience of suffering and insults that mysteriously he is to find his help. We note in these verses the servant's twice-expressed confidence in God (vv. 7 and 9).

So we come to the last, and the most challenging, of the four servant passages, Isaiah 52.13—53.12. This extended passage falls into six parts:

52.13–15	Opening speech by God
53.1–3	The sufferings of the servant
53.4–6	Healing and forgiveness
53.7–9	The fate of the servant
53.10–11b	The purpose of this
53.11c–12	Closing speech by God

The opening speech by God (52.13–15) offers a summary of what follows, namely that this servant was seen to be successful and was exalted. Yet before that happened many people were startled, astonished at his appearance, even going as far as despising him. Nevertheless, in the fulness of time they were forced to come to a very different assessment of who he was and what he had done.

Then 53.1–3 tells of the sufferings of the servant, this being voiced by an un-named group of people. Here they are referred to as 'we', and in all probability we should understand that they make up the same group as those who in 52.14–15 are called 'they'. Indeed, it would seem that these people, the 'we' of 53.1–3 and the 'they' of 52.14– 15, are those who come to the conclusion that 'he', the servant, the individual who is spoken about in every verse in the passage, has done something for them that they could not do for themselves. Through what 'he' has done, 'we'/'they' have been the fortunate beneficiaries.

That is the point made in 53.4–6, that the 'we' have received healing by his, the servant's, bruises. It is he who has carried their diseases, been wounded for their transgressions. The earlier assessment on the part of these unnamed speakers concerning the servant was that he, the servant, had been stricken by God, struck down by God and afflicted. In this we must assume that their thoughts were going along those traditional lines, as represented by the so-called comforters of Job, the central figure of the Old Testament book bearing his name, namely that Job's sufferings must have been caused by his own sin and the resulting punishment of God. While Job says that he cannot accept that, yet the book of Deuteronomy avers that if only the people of Israel will do the will of God, and walk in his ways, then all will be well. Similarly those who do not do the will of God will be subject to the judgement of God (see, for example, Deuteronomy 28). It would seem that it is this sort of traditional thought that lies behind that earlier assessment of the unnamed speakers as regards the servant and his sufferings. Yet they come to change their minds, coming to understand that their first reaction to him was both hasty and superficial. Perhaps it was after thought and deliberation that they came to their new understanding, namely,

> But he was wounded for our transgressions,
>> crushed for our iniquities;
> upon him was the punishment that made us whole,
>> and by his bruises we are healed.
> All we like sheep have gone astray;
>> we have all turned to our own way,
> and the Lord has laid on him
>> the iniquity of us all. (Isaiah 53.5–6)

Now the last two lines of that remind us of the ritual of the scapegoat that was part of the ceremonies on the Day of Atonement, spoken about in Leviticus 16. In this ritual the sins of the people were ceremonially laid upon the head of a goat which was then driven to a solitary place far away. Here, so it was believed, was one means by which sins were removed – by God. But it has to be said that the Old Testament nowhere else other than in Isaiah 53.6 knows of a *human being* having been appointed to carry away sins.

The passage continues in 53.7-9, speaking of the fate of the servant. In a quiet and calm spirit, without protest, he accepted all that was happening to him. At one level, and this is brought out in verse 8, this appeared to be a 'perversion of justice', but at a deeper level, and this too is brought out in the same verse, there is the affirmation that the servant's being stricken was 'for the transgression of my people'. Verse 9 would seem to make it clear that the servant did actually die, a death that would appear to be 'unfair', lacking justice, in fact 'a perversion of justice' (v. 8),[64] yet ends with the affirmation that the servant himself had done no violence, nor was he deceitful.

Thus we come to Isaiah 53.10–11b which speaks about the purpose of this death of the servant, that in fact it was God's will that *he* should suffer, not in any insignificant or unmeaningful way, but rather so that his life might be made 'an offering for sin'. Now these words of verse 10 (here in the rendering of the NRSV) represent the Hebrew *'asham*, frequently translated 'guilt offering', and spoken about in Leviticus 6.1–26; 7.1–10; Ezekiel 40.39 and elsewhere. It was a sacrifice offered so that certain sins might be forgiven, but in no other part of the Old Testament is there any thought of a human life being the offering in such a sacrifice. Normally a goat or a sheep would be offered, or for those of little wealth, a turtle dove or a pigeon.

The closure of this remarkable passage comes in 53.11c–12, in the form of a speech by God, but as so often in this whole piece the Hebrew is not easy to understand and thus to translate. However, the last line of verse 11 is reasonably straightforward with its, 'and he shall bear their iniquities'. Thus once again, here is the concept of the servant as the sacrificial offering through which the sins of others are forgiven. When we come to verse 12, the theme is the future exaltation of the servant, who will 'divide the spoil with the strong'. That is, it is stated that for him there is life after death, though how that is to take place, and what form it will take, we are not told. While life after death is spoken about, there is no mention of 'resurrection'. And the conclusion to the whole passage is a repeat of the most startling fact that has been uttered here:

> Yet he bore the sin of many,
>   and made intercession for the transgressors.
>
> (Isaiah 53.12)

There is nothing else like this in the Old Testament, and thus nothing with which we may compare it, nothing to consult to see if light can be shed from another quarter upon its new and radical words. What *is* clear is that here there is talk of the offering of a life for the sins of others. That is, by the offering of the life of the servant others may live. And further, all this is due to the will of God, and, it should be added, through the acceptance of this on the part of the servant.

Who is this servant who is being spoken about here? In particular, is this passage about Jesus? It is possible – even tempting – for Christians to read this as a prophecy about Jesus. Further, Christians would want to say that these words were fulfilled, remarkably fulfilled, in the events of Jesus' death on the cross and his subsequent resurrection from the dead. But is this what the prophet was thinking about when, under God, he wrote these words? Who can know the mind of the prophet? This we cannot know, and yet an educated guess may not be unreasonable. There are Christians who say that it is Jesus who is being spoken about here. Yet while I would not in any way deny that these words of the prophet found a remarkable fulfillment in Jesus, I have yet to be convinced that the prophet was actually seeing Jesus here, believing himself to be writing about Jesus. After all, we are talking about a prophet who it seems lived some five hundred years before the birth of Jesus (some seven hundred if there was only one prophet of the book of Isaiah!), and I see this prophet as intending to speak to, and thereby address, his people for a much more immediate situation than that. I understand this prophet as saying things that had come to him out of his experience of the time in exile in Babylon, what became for him a time of enforced life in a much wider world than anything he and his fellow people had known before, and a life that, comparatively speaking, lacked the old freedoms and political independence, power and prestige. Yet I see this prophet as having come to understand and to appreciate the presence and the ongoing purposes of God in all these harsh and unexpected experiences. It was an appreciation that God's way may be known, that his will may be done, in and through conditions of human weakness and loss of prestige as much, if not more, than in conditions and settings of human power and authority. This prophet had understood that the days of empire for Israelite people had gone, but that the day of the servant had come, that the days of a concentrated life in a small self-contained nation state had gone, but that the day of being a people within and part of a much greater whole had come, and come to stay. Thus the day of world mission and servanthood had come. In all this he perceived the presence and purpose of the Lord.

So I wish to argue that the servant in the first place is not Jesus, though Christians do of course find Isaiah 52.13—53.12 remarkably fulfilled in the life, work, death and resurrection of Jesus. Further, I do not think that we have to force all these four passages (42.1–4; 49.1–6; 50.4–9; 52.13—53.12) into a presentation of one particular servant. I suggest that there never was intended to be a solution to the mystery of the servant along those lines. Rather, here are four pictures of how it will be for the people of God in the future, no longer living as victors, enjoying the fruits of victory and the spoils of war, but much more as humble people, no doubt under the domination of a foreign power, with a mission to fulfil, others to witness to, to suffer with and suffer for, maybe even to give life – perhaps individual, perhaps corporate – that others may have life and may experience all the blessings that flow from life lived under the care of and in covenant relationship with God.

And that, in fact, was the way that in the fulness of time it turned out to be. The way of service and suffering was not just the way for the one, but was also to be the way for the many. Not only did Jesus have to take the way of suffering, but his followers too.

> Then he [Jesus] began to teach them that the Son of Man
> must undergo great suffering, and be rejected by the
> elders, the chief priests, and the scribes, and be killed, and
> after three days rise again.... He called the crowd with his
> disciples, and said to them, 'If any want to become my
> followers, let them deny themselves and take up their
> cross and follow me.' (Mark 8.31, 34)

It is time to move on from these startling and remarkable four
passages about servanthood, and turn to the last two chapters of
this part of the book of Isaiah. The ringing theme of Isaiah 54
and 55 is that the will and purposes of God *will* find fulfilment.
We should not think, however, that the servant theme is now forgotten. Much more, servanthood is henceforth to be understood
as part and parcel of the purposes of God, purposes which his
people may be sure will take place. Thus 54.1–10 is a joyful celebration of the great increase in population that will occur in
Jerusalem as the exiles return home. Zion, Jerusalem, is here
imagined, personified first as a barren woman with no children,
but assured that she will come to have more children than many
a married one (v. 1). Therefore, let those concerned be ready and
prepared for the necessary expansion of the city (vv. 2–3)! So will
all discouragement be shaken off, for the city is destined no longer
to be deserted.

> Do not fear, for you will not be ashamed;
>> do not be discouraged, for you will not suffer
>>> disgrace;
> for you will forget the shame of your youth,
>> and the disgrace of your widowhood you will
>>> remember no more.
> For your Maker is your husband,
>> the Lord of hosts is his name;
> the Holy One of Israel is your Redeemer,
>> the God of the whole earth he is called.

> For the Lord has called you
>> like a wife forsaken and grieved in spirit,
> like the wife of a man's youth when she is cast off,
>> says your God.
> For a brief moment I abandoned you,
>> but with great compassion I will gather you.
> In overflowing wrath for a moment
>> I hid my face from you,
> but with everlasting love I will have compassion on you,
>> says the Lord, your Redeemer. (Isaiah 54.4–8)

And how dependably sure will be the ongoing presence and peace of God for his people.

> For the mountains may depart
>> and the hills be removed,
> but my steadfast love shall not depart from you,
>> and my covenant of peace shall not be removed,
>> says the Lord, who has compassion on you.
> (Isaiah 54.10)

And all this leads on to the great transformation that will take place for the city, in that it will be both beautifully transformed and marvellously protected (54.11–17).

So the thrilling prophecies of the so-called Second Isaiah come to an end with chapter 55, a chapter that so much sums up the message of those that precede. Let the people come to the Lord and let them freely receive all that he has for them (55.1–5), and let them seize the opportunity that they are now being given. Let them go forth in joy and peace, rejoicing in being a part of a whole new creation, its various parts bursting into song and resonating with clapping.

> For you shall go out in joy,
>> and be led back in peace;
> the mountains and hills before you
>> shall burst into song,

and all the trees of the field shall clap their hands.
Instead of the thorn shall come up the cypress;

    instead of the brier shall come up the myrtle;
and it shall be to the Lord for a memorial,

    for an everlasting sign that shall not be cut off.
(Isaiah 55.12–13)[65]

III

CHAPTERS 56 TO 66

Here is another of those sudden changes that we come to in the book of Isaiah, akin to the one at the beginning of chapter 40. But here is a change in the opposite direction from the one between chapters 39 and 40, in that while that was a dramatic change from sombre note to thrilling and hopeful message, this one is from all creation's excitement at the new things that God is about to do for his people who are in exile in Babylon (55.12–13) to the beginning of something that looks much more restrained and cautious.

> Thus says the Lord:
>> maintain justice, and do what is right,
> for soon my salvation will come,
>> and my deliverance be revealed. (Isaiah 56.1)

It has long been suggested that the original historical setting of Isaiah 56 to 66 is that of the restored Jewish community in Jerusalem after returning from exile in Babylon and elsewhere. That is a generally accepted view, and is the one followed in this present work. Yet having said that, we have to accept our lack of certainty as regards a good number of the details. What we have in these chapters is, as we shall come to see, remarkably varied material that certainly does not display the homogeneity of chapters 40 to 55. Such variety in content leads us to believe that it is the work of a number of authors, even a number of prophets. It has to be said that our knowledge of historical details concerning the life of the post-exilic Jerusalem community is both scarce and patchy, which means that it is not easy to relate particular parts of these chapters to particular historical events. While a wide range of dates has been suggested for this material – from as early as 538 and 519 BC, and some parts even coming from pre-exilic times, to as late as the third century BC – the working hypothesis for this book is that these chapters are the work of a number of authors who wrote in the time after the exile, quite probably soon after the exile.[66]

The literary style – by which I mean the style of writing – that we find in these chapters is also varied. We have passages that contain prophetic words of condemnation of both people and practices, which read rather like the denunciations of the prophets who prophesied in the days before the exile. Hence, the suggestion has been made that they do come from pre-exilic times, and yet equally it can be argued that they come from the setting of the restored community in Jerusalem in the days after the exile. Examples of these are Isaiah 56.9—57.13 and 65.1–16. Then there are passages about the forthcoming glory of Jerusalem (much of chapters 60 to 62), there is an anguished prayer of lament (63.7—64.12), a passage that looks uncommonly like a sermon (59.1–21), passages which, as will be spelled out in what follows, have some startling and radical things to say (56.1–8), thrilling pictures of pilgrims and outcasts coming to make Jerusalem their new, or renewed, home (56.8; 62.1–12), the assurance that in the end there will be God and that he will deal with all that is opposed to his will (63.1–6).

Then as far as the theological thought of these chapters is concerned we find here the same basic concerns of God and his relationships with people, and the place of the city of Jerusalem within that nexus of relationships and in the purposes of God. However, the situation for all those relationships is now different, and thus what is being said has a somewhat different slant put upon it from the one we found in the preceding chapters. Then further, a variety of words are now used with rather different meanings, and in rather different senses, from what they had in chapters 40 to 55. Thus, for example, while 'deliverance' and 'salvation' in chapters 40 to 55 are deliverance and being saved from exile, here in chapters 56 to 66 they are from oppression (56.1;

61.10–11). Moreover, a characteristic feature of the later Old Testament prophetical material, such as these chapters along with what we have in Malachi, Zechariah 9 to 14 and Joel, is that it appears to be less tied to particular events and more concerned with themes and institutions.[67]

Almost all of the themes taken up in these chapters, and most of the concerns and institutions spoken about, find a mention in the opening eight verses, 56.1–8, and it is to these that I now turn. I shall take these a verse or two at a time and speak about the issues raised in them and about how they are developed in the chapters that follow. The exception to this will be chapter 66 which, because it seems intended to fill a particular function as the last chapter of the whole book, will be considered after we have given thought to 56.1–8.

Chapter 56, verses 1–8: Servants of God

Isaiah 56 to 66 opens with two verses which deal with three themes.

> Thus says the Lord:
>   Maintain justice, and do what is right,
> for soon my salvation will come,
>   and my deliverance be revealed.
> Happy is the mortal who does this,
>   the one who holds it fast,
> who keeps the sabbath, not profaning it,
>   and refrains from doing any evil. (Isaiah 56.1–2)

The three issues spoken about here are (1) maintaining justice, doing what is right, and refraining from evil; (2) salvation, deliverance; and (3) sabbath. But in the first place we need to say something about the speaker in these verses, and in fact in all of this passage (56.1–8), that is, the Lord (v. 1). In my commentary on Isaiah 40–66 I argued that the three principal themes in all the main parts of the book of Isaiah are God, his people, and Jerusalem. In these present chapters God is spoken of as the Holy One of Israel (60.9, 14) as he is in other parts of the book. His dwelling is in heaven (58.4; 63.15; 66.1–2), in a high and lofty place (57.15; with which we may compare 6.1–13), and he desires to bring deliverance to his people (56.1; 61.10–11). Rather differently from elsewhere in the Old Testament the Lord here bears the name 'Amen' (65.15b–16 [NRSV, 'faithfulness']). In 63.16 and 64.8 he is referred to as 'our Father'.[68] It should also be mentioned at this point that there is a particular monotheistic emphasis in Isaiah 56 to 66, that there is only one God. Any cultic practices in connection with any other deities here receive the sharpest criticism and condemnation (see especially 57.3–13). Rather, let his people put their whole trust in the Lord who ever and with all his might works to banish their enemies (63.1–6), and also those among their own people who do not act with justice towards others (59.15b–19).

We can now turn to the three main issues which are spoken about in the Lord's address to his people in 56.1–8.

(1) In Isaiah 56 to 66 there is a real emphasis on morality, the importance of God's people leading ethically good lives. Thus the very first word spoken by the Lord through his prophet here in 56.1–8 concerns maintaining justice and doing what is right (v. 1), and at the same time refraining from evil (v. 2). Further, we observe that the issue recurs a significant number of times in these chapters. In the anguished prayer in 63.7—64.12 there is the crying out to God from a situation in which there is evil and lack of justice; in 56.9–12 there is talk of corrupt leaders; in 65.1–16 the warning of the judgement of God upon human rebellion; in 63.1–6 the most threatening scene of the holy God's coming in judgement upon those who are opposed to him. Rather, those who are close to God are the humble, not the wicked (57.14–21). What is required of the wicked is that they come before God in confession.

> For our transgressions before you are many,
>   and our sins testify against us.
> Our transgressions indeed are with us,
>   and we know our iniquities:
> transgressing, and denying the Lord,

> and turning away from following our God,
> talking oppression and revolt,
> conceiving lying words and uttering them from
> the heart. (Isaiah 59.12–13)

In these chapters what is envisaged is that there will be faithful 'servants' of God. See, for example, 65.8–16a. Some students of these chapters maintain that 'servants' is one of the principal themes of Isaiah 56 to 66, even where the word is not actually used,[69] and there is much to be said for this view, and hence the title that I have adopted for the passage currently under consideration, 56.1–8. In this part of the book of Isaiah there is a presentation of 'servants of God', those who seek in their lives to live in faithfulness to the Lord, those who do indeed live in accordance with those visions set forth in the 'servant' passages in chapters 40 to 55 (Isaiah 42.1–4; 49.1–6; 50.4–9; 52.13—53.12).

(2) The second issue calling for discussion is 'salvation … deliverance'. These words occur earlier in the Isaiah book, for example in 46.13 where they were concerned with the purpose of the Lord to 'deliver' his people from their exile in Babylon; in that sense to bring them 'salvation'. Here in chapters 56 to 66 these words are used in the sense that deliverance and fulness of life will come through the practice of the devout and moral life in the re-established community of God's people in Jerusalem. What we are witnessing here are changes in the meaning of certain words and concepts in the book of Isaiah, as here between their usages in chapters 40 to 55 and 56 to 66. Such changes in the meaning of these words are reflective of the changing experiences and situations of the communities to which respectively the words were addressed.[70] The message that is being conveyed here through the words 'salvation' and 'deliverance' is that God desires wholeness of life for his people. Thus,

> And he will come to Zion as Redeemer,
> to those in Jacob who turn from transgression,
> says the Lord. (Isaiah 59.20)

The same divine will is there in the ministry of the one appointed and anointed by God, spoken about in chapter 61.

> The spirit of the Lord God is upon me,
>> because the Lord has anointed me;
> he has sent me to bring good news to the oppressed,
>> to bind up the broken-hearted,
> to proclaim liberty to the captives,
>> and release to the prisoners;
> to proclaim the year of the Lord's favour,
>> and the day of vengeance of our God;
>> to comfort all who mourn;
> to provide for those who mourn in Zion –
>> to give them a garland instead of ashes,
> the oil of gladness instead of mourning,
>> the mantle of praise instead of a faint spirit.
> They will be called oaks of righteousness,
>> the planting of the Lord, to display his glory.
> (Isaiah 61.1–3)

(3) In the third place sabbath is spoken about in 56.2 and this subject calls for some comment. Although the institution and observance of sabbath is spoken about in parts of the Old Testament that purport to be concerned with times prior to exile, it does seem that it was with the fall of Jerusalem and the destruction of the temple that sabbath took on new meaning and importance, becoming a day that in its faithful observance was a principal mark of those who were Jewish and who embraced the historic faith of the Israelite people. Celebration of the sabbath, along with such practices as circumcision, became one of the distinctive features of the Jewish community, and of those – as we shall come to see – who joined themselves to that community. However, in Isaiah 56 to 66 there is nothing about circumcision as a mark of those who are part of the community of faith; the only condition for admission to the community here is sabbath observance. Thus there is spoken about here in 56.2 that sense of blessedness and joy in the faithful observance of the sabbath:

> Happy is the mortal who does this,
>> the one who holds it fast,
> who keeps the sabbath, not profaning it,
>> and refrains from doing any evil. (Isaiah 56.2)

Further references to sabbath in these chapters are found in 56.4; 58.13 and 66.23.

We move on to Isaiah 56.3-5 and note immediately the emphasis on foreigners and eunuchs, matters we need to consider here. These verses read as follows.

> Do not let the foreigner joined to the Lord say,
>> 'The Lord will surely separate me from his people';
> and do not let the eunuch say,
>> 'I am just a dry tree.'
> For thus says the Lord:
> To the eunuchs who keep my sabbaths,
>> who choose the things that please me
>> and hold fast my covenant,
> I will give, in my house and within my walls,
>> a monument and a name
>> better than sons and daughters;
> I will give them an everlasting name
>> that shall not be cut off. (Isaiah 56.3–5)

The main point that we need to understand about what is being said here is that both foreigners and eunuchs are being welcomed into the community of God's people. The 'foreigners' were those who were converts to Judaism, proselytes, those who wished to become part of the Jewish people. Here is something of the fulfilment of that vision of internationalism set forth in chapters 40 to 55 (see especially 44.3–5). These 'foreigners' were here being welcomed into the fellowship of God's people, though it has to be said that there do seem to have been other voices raised in the post-exilic community, ones that were more questioning and cautious about the admission of such people (see for example Ezra 4.1–3).

No doubt what we have in Isaiah 56 to 66 is something that came out of the experience of living in the much wider and more international world of the Babylonian, and other exiles, situations that were very different for Israelite people from anything that they had experienced hitherto. Equally we can understand that the arrival of such foreigners in Jerusalem in those times would give rise to a variety of responses on the part of those who historically had made up the Lord's people. Nevertheless, the stance taken in Isaiah 56 to 66 in this regard is clear enough to us – and should have been clear enough to those to whom it was originally addressed.

The second group of people spoken about in these verses is the eunuchs, those Jewish and non-Jewish people who had been sexually mutilated so that they could serve in certain parts of the Babylonian, and later Persian, imperial service. One thinks in particular of service in the imperial harems, and we may recall that note of warning in the somewhat warm words of Isaiah to Hezekiah after the king had confessed to showing to the Babylonian envoys all that was in his house, all the contents of his storehouses – 'Some of your own sons who are born to you shall be taken away; they shall be eunuchs in the palace of the king of Babylon' (Isaiah 39.7). Further, we need to bear in mind that parts of the Old Testament such as Deuteronomy 23.1 strictly exclude such people from membership of the religious community, yet here they are being welcomed. Again, we can well imagine the situation in the post-exilic community brought about by the presence of such people, and we can equally well imagine the different reactions and responses that it drew forth. The fact is that this community found itself in this, and also in other regards, as being in a new and different situation that demanded careful thought as to appropriate responses. Neither for the first nor the last time were the responses varied and different! Yet again, the stance taken in, and by those responsible for, Isaiah 56 to 66 is clear enough.

So to Isaiah 56.6–7, verses which bring to our notice first the holy mountain, Jerusalem, and then second the temple that was intended to have a central place in the city, and those who were qualified to minister in it. The verses concerned read as follows:

> And the foreigners who join themselves to the Lord,
>> to minister to him, to love the name of the Lord,
>> and to be his servants,
> all who keep the sabbath, and do not profane it,
>> and hold fast my covenant –
> these I will bring to my holy mountain,
>> and make them joyful in my house of prayer;
> their burnt-offerings and their sacrifices
>> will be accepted on my altar;
> for my house shall be called a house of prayer
>> for all peoples. (Isaiah 56.6–7)

We begin with the reference in verse 7 above to God's holy mountain, that is Mount Zion, that is the city of Jerusalem. Within chapters 56 to 66 there is a real emphasis upon the fact that the city is to be rebuild and that it will moreover be most gloriously restored. Isaiah 60.1-22 speaks glowingly of the new glory of Jerusalem, and the theme continues in chapters 61 and 62. Together these chapters make up the central section of this part of the book of Isaiah, and they are marked by a profound spirit of hopefulness, so much so that we are able to see similarities in what is being said here with parts of chapters 40 to 55. This city of peace will have gates that will ever be open (60.11), glorious and precious materials will be used in its rebuilding (60.17), it will be a place where salvation is experienced and praise made (60.18), city and land shall no longer be called 'Forsaken' and 'Desolate', but instead 'My Delight is in Her' and 'Married' (62.4). As for the people of this city they will be named 'The Holy People, The Redeemed of the Lord' and the city itself 'Sought Out, A City Not Forsaken' (62.12).

Then there is the matter of the house, the temple. In Isaiah 61.4 we are given a picture of a city still in a ruinous state, and most likely the ruined temple was part of that. Isaiah 64.11 seems to suggest that the temple is still a burnt-out ruin. Perhaps, then, we should think of 56.6–7 as being in the nature of sketch plans and ideas for the future. These envisage that sacrifices and offerings will be made; there is the vision that those institutions will be restored, but that they will be made radically new in that the gifts and sacrifices of the foreigners will be accepted, indeed welcomed (see also 60.7), and even that the ministrations of foreigners will be accepted. This last aspect is confirmed by Isaiah 66.21 which says about those who are gathered in from nations far away, 'I will also take some of them as priests and as Levites, says the Lord'. This is a real working out of what Blenkinsopp calls the 'open admissions policy' expressed in Isaiah 56 to 66.[71] Further, and it would appear very much along the lines spoken about in Solomon's prayer at the dedication of the temple he had built (1 Kings 8.14–61),[72] that the new post-exilic temple would be a place of prayer – and a place of prayer, we note, 'for all peoples' (Isaiah 56.7).

So we come to Isaiah 56.8, which reads:

> Thus says the Lord God,
> who gathers the outcasts of Israel,
> I will gather others to them
> besides those already gathered.

Thrillingly, it is the Lord who is here portrayed as taking the initiative in gathering the outcasts of Israel from the various places where they had become scattered in the crises of 598 and 587 BC, and joining them in Zion with those already gathered, though just who these latter are, where they have come from, and any national identity that they may have had are left unstated. However, we have already had promises of such happenings spoken about in the book of Isaiah at 11.12 and 43.5–6. Childs reminds us of the close parallel that we find in the New Testament in John 10.16 which has, 'a similar openness to the further ingathering, but with a purposefully undefined referent'.[73] But in the immediate post-exilic context the basic promise and theme is spelled out in chapter 60. It is as if the motto theme is sounded in verse 3,

Nations shall come to your light,
    and kings to the brightness of your dawn. (Isaiah 60.3)

Then in 60.4–9 the details are spelled out, the fugue is being
played on the motto theme. These people are to be both those
who are Jewish and also those who are not. They will come both
by land and also by sea. They will come with great wealth that will
contribute to the future glorification of the city, and presumably
to that of the yet to be rebuilt temple – the abundance of the sea,
the wealth of the nations (v. 5), gold and frankincense (v. 6). And
we should perhaps take particular note of verse 7 with its assurance that the sacrificial offerings of foreigners will be accepted in
the new Temple.

All the flocks of Kedar shall be gathered to you,
    the rams of Nebaioth shall minister to you;
they shall be acceptable on my altar,
    and I will glorify my glorious house. (Isaiah 60.7)

What is an inevitable, and in fact essential, part of all this is the
great reversal of fortunes for the people of Israel and their erstwhile enemies. This is a theme that has earlier been sounded
(Isaiah 45.14; 49.22–23), and here involves the city of Jerusalem
being given a new name by those who had earlier despised it.

The descendants of those who oppressed you
    shall come bending low to you,
and all who despised you
    shall bow down at your feet;
they shall call you the City of the Lord,
    the Zion of the Holy One of Israel. (Isaiah 60.14)

And there, in that verse, is the last occurrence of what in the book
of Isaiah is the especially characteristic expression for the Lord,
that is, the Holy One of Israel. Here it is linked with the name of
the city, Zion, and thus in this verse are brought together the
three main themes of the whole book, the Lord, his people, and
the city of Jerusalem. Here are Lord, people and city all being

spoken about in this new situation following the return from exile, now in very changed circumstances indeed from those of earlier ages, and yet still in ongoing purpose and pilgrimage, themes that have in this remarkable book of Isaiah been explored in a variety of ages, settings and conditions.

Chapter 66: Judgement and salvation

An imaginary Dr Watson-like figure might find himself or herself confused over the apparent lack of logical connections between the various parts of Isaiah 66. Our, also imaginary, Sherlock Holmesian figure – that is with his biblical-studies hat on – might retort that the solution to the problem is indeed elementary (from the Latin, *elementa*, beginnings), in that if we go back to the beginning and look at chapter 1 of Isaiah then we shall observe (Holmes, we may remember, was critical of Watson for 'seeing' but not 'observing') that a series of similar, and at times identical, words are used in both the opening and the closing chapters of the book. It is surely reasonable to draw the conclusion that chapter 66 has been quite deliberately composed so as to stand in a particular relationship with chapter 1. We have already observed that Isaiah 1 bears the appearance of having been composed as an introduction to what follows it in the book of Isaiah, and to that we now add the further observation that 66 bears the appearance of having been composed in order to complete the book. Further, we find in chapter 66 some of the vocabulary and expressions employed in 40 to 55, and even more that there are echoes here of some of the main themes of 56 to 66. So perhaps there is a concern here in chapter 66 to do a number of things, namely to speak of the fulfilment of the thrilling message of 40 to 55, to do something to summarise the themes of 56 to 66, and to provide a satisfactory conclusion to the whole book. That, at any rate, is the working hypothesis that I adopt in my treatment now of chapter 66. [74]

The chapter opens in verses 1–4 with concern over a triad of related subjects, the dwelling place of God, the Jerusalem temple, and offering sacrifices to God. The true dwelling place of God is nothing less than heaven and earth (66.1), those terms reminding us of their employment in Isaiah 1.2. If and when there is to be once again a temple in Jerusalem it will certainly not be a dwelling place for God (66.1)! We assume that the thought is that it will rather be a place of prayer for his people (compare Isaiah 56.7). In verses 2–3 the concern is that worship and life go together to make up a seamless whole, matters that are emphasised in various parts of the book of Isaiah, especially in chapters 1 to 39 and 56 to 66. These issues are first spoken about in the book at Isaiah 1.12–17. When there is no true worship, then those supposed and so-called 'devotions' will not save the deluded devotees from the judgement of God (66.4).

Isaiah 66.5–6 contrasts two groups of people, both of which we have already encountered in the Isaiah book, again especially in chapters 1 to 39 and 56 to 66, namely those who are faithful to God and those who are not. The former group are those who, literally, 'tremble at his word'. The expression has already occurred in 66.2, and elsewhere in the Old Testament in Ezra 9.4 and 10.3, and would seem to indicate people who seek to be faithful to God. Blenkinsopp considers that the expression is used in chapters 56 to 66 as an alternative designation for God's 'servants'.[75] Meanwhile, the latter group is here given a solemn warning of imminent divine judgement, as if its arrival is being announced from the temple (v. 6).

The following verses, 66.7–14, are about the future glorification of Jerusalem, and have the image of the city as a mother of many children. This takes up the theme already spoken of in 49.18–23 and 54.1–3. Once again we read about the city that earlier was being mourned over, but now about which there is much rejoicing (see in chapters 40 to 55: 49.13; 51.11; 54.1 and in 56–66: 60.20; 61.1–11; 65.18–19). In verses 12–14 there is more about the new glory, prosperity and peace of Zion, expressed in a series of words that have already been employed in the Isaiah book, such as 'comfort', 'babes carried', 'wealth of nations'.[76]

So we come to 66.15–18a where the talk is of God's coming either in judgement on the sinners or to save those who are faithful. Some of the matters spoken about here are those highlighted earlier in the book – see 13.3–16; 17.12–14; 29.6; 30.27–28; 34.1–17; 65.6–7. Then in 66.18b–21 the universalistic note is sounded again, that which we have already heard in 42.5–9; 56.1–8; 61.6 and elsewhere.[77]

So we come to the last three verses of the book of Isaiah, which have a real power both to thrill and also to shock us – or at least to make us sit up and take notice. Verses 22 and 23 are thrilling, telling as they do of the permanence not only of the new heavens and the new earth (which have already been spoken about in 65.17) but also of 'your descendants and your name'. Now we have already heard about these 'descendants' and the 'name' in 65.9 and 15, and the clear impression is that they are those, or at least some of those, who are faithful to the Lord and who remain so. Indeed, they would appear to be the same faithful ones who elsewhere are called 'tremblers' (66.2, 5) or 'servants' (56.6; 63.17; 65.8, 9, 13–15). Thus with this mention of these people, these groups, we are witnessing in this chapter something of a summing up of the message of chapters 56 to 66, and we are also hearing something of an echo of words found in chapters 40 to 55, namely,

> Your offspring would have been like the sand,
> > and your descendants like its grains;
> their name would never be cut off
> > or destroyed from before me. (Isaiah 48.19)[78]

In 66.23 we are given a thrilling picture of true and ongoing worship of God by 'all flesh', the note of universalism making itself heard once again, that note that we have heard sounded not only in chapters 40 to 55, also in 56 to 66, and even in parts of 1 to 39 (for example, 2.2–4; 19.18–25). Here it is again, and here at this climactic moment in the whole book of Isaiah serving to emphasise and sum up what in this regard has gone before.

> From new moon to new moon,
> > and from sabbath to sabbath,
> all flesh shall come to worship before me,
> > says the Lord. (Isaiah 66.23)[79]

And 'all flesh' is there again in the very last verse of the book, 66.24. But what are we to make of this verse?

> And they shall go out and look at the dead bodies of the people who have rebelled against me; for their worm shall not die, their fire shall not be quenched, and they shall be an abhorrence to all flesh. (Isaiah 66.24)

Those who go out and see this ghastly sight would seem to be the faithful servants of God who have just been spoken about. What they see is indeed ghastly and gruesome, and its presence here gives a terrible ending to the book. In the Jewish church as this passage was read at the sabbath that coincided with the new moon it has been the practice to repeat verse 23 after verse 24, thus making the end of the book easier, more palatable. No small number of scholars have recorded their regret about, or difficulty with, this last verse of the book, frequently observing that it is because of the presence of this uncompromising verse that the book ends on a note far distant from earlier parts that displayed such great spiritual insight and elevated thought.

Understandable though that approach is, even so the ending of the book surely needs to be left as we find it. For this great work that comes to us from centuries ago deals with the eternal problem of the world's sin and that of individual people. We can see all too plainly that human sin and failure are here present on so many of the pages of this book, and further, that the book has no solution to the problem of human sinfulness. It is true that forgiveness is spoken about, but there is no dealing in any final way with sin. That would have to wait for the fulfillment of the ages, so Christians believe, until God himself came and acted. Meanwhile, there is the divine call to walk in the ways of God, even though all who seek to do that find themselves as part of the continuing sinful humanity. 'Therefore,' says B. S. Childs at the close of his one-volume commentary on the book of Isaiah, 'we still pray with the saints of every generation: "Maranatha, come quickly Lord Jesus."' [80] Indeed, with saints past and present we shall still sing,

O come, O come, Immanuel,
And ransom captive Israel,
That mourns in lonely exile here
Until the Son of God appear:
   Rejoice! Rejoice! Immanuel
   Shall come to thee, O Israel. [81]

INTERMEZZO

The book completed and ready to be opened

So there, as have seen in the foregoing pages, is the book of Isaiah
in all its variety and length, in its spread both in range of thought
and variety of literary expression, but also in the large historical
time span covered in that telling. It is one of the longest books in
the Old Testament, only rivalled by the book of Psalms. It is, further, one of the most complex books in the Hebrew Scriptures, in
that we have to work hard as we search for the logical connections
between the various parts of the whole.[1] Yet as we have seen in
the foregoing it is possible to discern a real sense of logic within
the whole arrangement of the book, a logic that we surely have
to say is owed not only to various prophetic authors (or preachers)
but also to editors, redactors who between them worked over a
considerable number of generations to produce what has come
down to us as the book of Isaiah. Christopher Seitz has given us
a rather brilliant illustration to describe this edited, redacted book
of Isaiah. In this 'parable' he is speaking of a 'redacted' house.
He says,

> I once lived in an old single-story farmhouse in the North
> Carolina countryside. One of the many interesting things
> about the house was its construction. From the outside it
> had a standard rectangular form that seemed in no way
> unusual. But the years and the weather revealed a secret
> the external form had hidden. Upon entering the central
> hall, it was clear that the right side of the house had set-
> tled more than the left. Further investigation indicated
> that a main portion of a rear interior wall was actually
> covered with exterior siding. In fact, there was even a full

sash window in the original building, facing out onto the interior space. Deduction: three or more houses had been combined to form our farmhouse.[2]

Application: all this sounds remarkably like the book of Isaiah, a book that quite distinctly reveals to us its different earlier parts,[3] but which also displays equally distinct evidences of having been deliberately put together to serve some purpose. We may further say that as the final builders of the farmhouse believed that there was worth in giving continuing usage to the earlier buildings, but that parts would have to be changed, altered, adapted for their ongoing employment, so also did the redactors of the book of Isaiah believe that the earlier materials they had inherited from the preaching of the various prophets and others – Isaiah, so-called Second Isaiah, and others, both prophets and editors – should be preserved for the future life, edification, encouragement of the people of God, but that they needed at least some adaptation and up-dating so as to serve in another age, or ages.

How, then, did the book reach its final form? By what means, and in what stages did this take place? There has been no dearth of proposals set forth to explain the various stages by which the book of Isaiah was built up until it eventually assumed its present form.[4] However, all these proposals are inevitably speculative, for in truth we have no real evidence about the stages of that process of growth. While we can see a number of clearly distinct blocks of material – what we might call the 'building blocks' – that eventually were joined together and so fashioned into the book of Isaiah that we know, yet we have to confess our ignorance about the actual processes and stages whereby the final work came into being. I have little doubt that it was a long process, that it took place over a good number of decades, and further that it took place in stages, but I have to say that the various detailed proposals of those who believe they can set out those stages, and their possible dates, seem to me to be too speculative to be convincing. Nor, I suggest, do we know whether or not that major block of material in chapters 40 to 55 ever existed as a written document in its own right before it became combined with some earlier part, or already combined parts, of the book. The same goes for those other major blocks such as chapters 56 to 66, 24 to 27, 33 to 39. Moreover, in all probability each of those three major blocks of material had their own individual histories and stages of growth until they became the chapters 24 to 27, 33 to 39 and 56 to 66 that we read.

Yet, as we have seen there are particular themes that run throughout the book, particular in vocabulary and expressions of language that, as we have observed, occur in various parts of it. Such considerations lead us to the conclusion that the work on the various parts of what eventually became the book of Isaiah was carried out by a succession of those who saw themselves as standing in the tradition of Isaiah of Jerusalem, a succession of those who believed that the prophet's words were of great worth and that they should be recorded for posterity. As time went by further prophetic and editorial contributions were made in changed contemporary settings – most dramatically those experiences of being taken into, and later being released from, exile. These major upheavals, and many lesser ones, called for an element of up-dating and adaptation of the earlier prophecies and teachings, for the reason that those who had assumed this ongoing responsibility were aware that time did not stand still, that conditions changed, and that the word of the Lord to his people came inevitably with different emphases in the contexts of later historical and cultural settings and circumstances.

We may perhaps go some way to illustrate this by considering the monastic movement in the Christian Church and in particular how that developed through the insights and teachings of a succession of leaders over changing centuries. Antony the Copt (AD 251?–356) is generally regarded as the originator of monasticism, and while there were those who in establishing it in the West took over his teaching very much as it was, with Benedict (AD 480–543) we have a leader whose Rule was a serious attempt to adapt the earlier monastic legislation for European needs in a later age. Or we may consider the historical developments and changes that have taken place in the various monastic and other orders in the church, how for example Franciscans look back to St Francis of Assisi (AD 1181/2–1226) and yet have had to make changes and adaptations over the centuries to what their founder did and what he prescribed for his order. Or consider the Society of Jesus which, while looking to St Ignatius Loyola (AD 1491 or 1495–1556) as its founder, has changed and adapted in its mission in different parts of the world over the subsequent ages. John Wesley's Methodists are now in a series of very different churches, manifesting enormous variety, now being established in many parts of the world, inevitably having had to adapt with developments that have taken place over succeeding generations. They have had to be aware of changed and changing historical circumstances, and they have had to make their own adaptations of the original 'model' so to be able to have something appropriate in the context of their various local cultural settings, but which yet display a form of church life that bears some 'family' likeness and has those particular emphases that were proclaimed by their founder.

All this is to say that perhaps we may be able to imagine the existence of a succession of prophets and editors who continued to regard Isaiah of Jerusalem as an outstanding prophet of the Lord, whose work and insights were of such an order that they must be recorded for future use, but who as time went by, and historical and cultural conditions changed, needed to produce new prophecies and new work – yet in what we might call the 'Isaiah tradition' – so that a new generation of God's people might be served, might be challenged, might be encouraged. Perhaps the nearest words that we can find to describe such a succession of individuals with their 'family likeness', in their concern to maintain the 'Isaiah tradition', are 'disciples' and 'school', with however the very large proviso of admitting that we know nothing about how such people worked and what was the nature of their relationships with each other.[5]

What, however, is much clearer is the matter of dating the completed work. In this regard two factors are particularly significant. Isaiah is spoken about in the book we commonly call

Ecclesiasticus, or else The Wisdom of Jesus Ben (or Son of) Sirach. The author of this work, Ben Sirach, in 48.22–25 speaks of Isaiah, and the reference to the fact that Isaiah 'comforted the mourners in Zion' (Sirach 48.24) suggests that in Ben Sirach's day chapters 40 to 55 were already incorporated into the work, along with earlier parts that Ben Sirach refers to, such as 'In Isaiah's days the sun went backwards, /and he prolonged the life of the king' (Sirach 48.23, in reference to Isaiah 38.4–8). P. W. Skehan and A. A. Di Lella suggest that the date of publication of The Wisdom of Jesus Ben Sirach was about 180 BC, though others would date it later than that, say between 132 and 110 BC.[6] The other factor to bear in mind as regards the date of the completed book of Isaiah concerns the Qumran scrolls. Among the many scrolls and other manuscripts found in the caves at Qumran on the shore of the Dead Sea in the 1940s were two scrolls of Isaiah. Both of these were in what became known as Cave 1, and were thus given the designations 1QIs[a] and 1QIs[b]. It is generally considered that neither of these can be later than the first century BC, with some suggesting that they might come from as early as around 140 BC. Both of these scrolls represent the text of the full sixty-six chapters of the book of Isaiah. 1QIs[a] is a complete scroll of the book, while 1QIs[b], though imperfectly preserved, covers some forty-six chapters beginning at 7.22 and including most of chapters 38–66.[7] Thus it would seem that by at least around 100 BC, and possibly earlier, the complete sixty-six-chapter book of Isaiah was in existence.

What, then, can we say as regards the content and the overall themes of the book of Isaiah? Along with the other major prophetic collections in the Old Testament the book of Isaiah is concerned with the relationship of God and his people, and with his intentions for them. This, as set forth in the presentation in the book of Isaiah, is centred in a particular way on Jerusalem, even for that time when in various places of exile God's people are separated from the holy city. The book speaks of the holiness and otherness of the Lord, yet also of his special closeness to his people Israel. The rather special designation for God that finds particular employment in the Isaiah book is the 'Holy One of Israel', a title that speaks both of the Lord's essential otherness from the world and things of earth, but also of his special relationship with his people. Further, for and with these people the Lord has ongoing purposes. This is a great and ongoing reality even though in age after age these people are sinful and are apparently in near-continuous rebellion against the Lord's will for them. This sinfulness brings in its train God's holy judgement upon them, and yet also his forgiveness and his call to his people to engage in an ongoing pilgrimage. Amazingly, they are still required to be involved in his widening purposes. At one historical moment the truth for these sinful people about their future goes like this:

> It is too light a thing that you should be my servant
> > to raise up the tribes of Jacob
> > and to restore the survivors of Israel;
> I will give you as a light to to the nations,
> > that my salvation may reach to the end of the earth.
> (Isaiah 49.6)

For all this is to be lived out amidst the political realities of a changing world, and in this regard the Isaiah book leads us through a series of world eras, the Assyrian, the Babylonian and the Persian ages, and invites us to appreciate how new ages do both teach new duties and also beget new insights as to how the people of God are to be the people of God. One of the great movements through which the book leads us is the one from when the people of Judah and Jerusalem enjoyed political independence through to the time in which they were under the rule of a superior wordly power. Whereas at the beginning of the book we may have reference to various kings in Jerusalem – and also in Samaria – by the centre part of the book the predominant figure has become that of a servant. That surely was an insight that came out of the Jewish experience of being a captive people in exile and coming to see that their ongoing political situation would be one of subservience. In this experience they found a new presence and call of God, both alike appropriate for the new age and their own new situation. Yet we have to ask whether without these searing experiences would they, or at least some of them, have come to those new insights as to a more worldwide setting for their mission and the call of God's people to find in the way of suffering and servanthood their intended path to real life?

Here then in the book of Isaiah is the call to God's people to be faithful to him through a series of changing ages, conditions, and situations. They are counselled here to seek to live in his light and to walk in his ways, to live out their faith in their communities and in their world, to practise justice in their dealings with one another, to believe that their Lord as well as having a particular relationship with his ancient and ongoing people of Israel is also the Lord of all, and that in the fulness of time his purposes will prevail. Thus stands the promise enshrined in this remarkable book:

> On this mountain the Lord of hosts will make for all
> peoples
> a feast of rich food, a feast of well-matured wines,
> of rich food filled with marrow, of well-matured
> wines strained clear.
> And he will destroy on this mountain
> the shroud that is cast over all peoples,
> the sheet that is spread over all nations;
> he will swallow up death for ever.
> Then the Lord God will wipe away the tears from
> all faces,
> and the disgrace of his people he will take away from
> all the earth,
> for the Lord has spoken.
> It will be said on that day,
> Lo, this is our God; we have waited for him,
> so that he might save us.
> This is the Lord for whom we have waited;
> let us be glad and rejoice in his salvation.
> (Isaiah 25.6–9)

And why should we open this book and read it today? We should open it and read it because it takes us to great depths in our belief about God and his relationships with his people and his world. We should read it too for the length and breadth of its understanding of these things. It is of incalculable value for us in that it leads us through a succession of eras in the affairs of the world. In this book we are enabled, as it were, to lean over the shoulders of those who were caught up in those events and their changing scenarios, (or at least to look over the shoulders of those who passed on these things), and who in the light of their historic faith perforce had to make their responses, some for good but others, inevitably, for ill. For there are few people in the book of Isaiah who are paragons of virtue and faith: much more are they rather fallible and sinful beings like ourselves, all too often making clumsy movements in the world, all too often apparently bent on going in the least appropriate ways.

And nor for the most part were the leaders – and are the leaders – any much better, yet here in Isaiah is set forth the vision for the future of a truly good and godly ruler, who will be called,

> Wonderful Counsellor, Mighty God,
>   Everlasting Father, Prince of Peace.
> His authority shall grow continually,
>   and there shall be endless peace
> for the throne of David and his kingdom.
>   He will establish and uphold it
> with justice and with righteousness
>   from this time onwards and for evermore.
> The zeal of the Lord of hosts will do this.
> (Isaiah 9.6b–7)

That, however, was a word proclaimed in one historical moment, and it would have to be modified in the light of further and later experiences. To it would have to be added those insights that we are given in the four passages about servanthood (42.1–4; 49.1–6; 50.4–9; 52.13—53.12). Within them, as we have seen, is the great insight that would come to its destined fulfilment in the new dispensation inaugurated in the life and ministry, death and resurrection of Jesus, namely that the future way of life for God's people will have this theme of servanthood at its centre, the theme learned by at least one person (perhaps only by one person?) so painfully in all those dreadful experiences of destruction of the homeland and all its old securities and certainties, and learned also in the strange life of exile. At first all this seemed totally unaccountable, like the appearance of the so-called 'servant'.

> For he grew up before him like a young plant,
>   and like a root out of dry ground;
> he had no form or majesty that we should look at him,
>   nothing in his appearance that we should desire him.
> (Isaiah 53.2)

Yet in the medium term there could be meaning, though there was nothing startlingly new here.

> Is not this the fast that I choose:
>   to loose the bonds of injustice,
>   to undo the thongs of the yoke,
> to let the oppressed go free,
>   and to break every yoke?
> Is it not to share your bread with the hungry,
>   and bring the homeless poor into your house;
> when you see the naked, to cover them,
>   and not to hide yourself from your own kin?
> (Isaiah 58.6–7; compare 1.16–17; 5.7)

And, for the longer term, servanthood in even more demanding ways – and here *was* something new:

> Surely he has borne our infirmities
>   and carried our diseases;
> yet we accounted him stricken,
>   struck down by God, and afflicted.
> But he was wounded for our transgressions,
>   crushed for our iniquities;

upon him was the punishment that made us whole,
    and by his bruises we are healed.
All we like sheep have gone astray;
    we have all turned to our own way,
and the Lord has laid on him
    the iniquity of us all. (Isaiah 53.4–6)

Thus it is that although the book of Isaiah may have no immediate solution to the problem of the ever-present and all-pervading sinfulness of humanity, yet it must be said that within its pages there is this great insight for the future. It is an insight, a clue as to future ways, as here given expression (in English translation from the original Welsh) by William Williams of Pantycelyn.

Can I forget bright Eden's grace,
My beauteous crown and princely place,
    All lost, all lost to me?
Long as I live I'll praise and sing
My wondrous all-restoring King,
    Victor of Calvary.[8]

PART TWO

THE OPEN BOOK

I

THE KING IS DEAD!

LONG LIVE THE SERVANT!

'The time has come', Lewis Carroll's Walrus famously remarked, 'to talk of many things', and among those many things, as we all know, were kings. But as far as the book of Isaiah is concerned, the talk of kings is mainly in the first part of the book, that is in chapters 1 to 39. And if we restrict our talking to Israelite kings, then it is confined to chapters 1 to 39; from chapter 40 onwards there is no talk about an Israelite king. On the other hand in chapters 1 to 39 there are far fewer occurrences of the words 'servant' or 'servants' than there are in chapters 40 onwards. It is with this apparent imbalance of references to kings and servants in the book of Isaiah that I am concerned.

The book of Lamentations is a hauntingly sad book; it speaks of the tragedy of the fall of Jerusalem and the destruction of the temple:

> How lonely sits the city
>   that once was full of people!
> How like a widow she has become,
>   she that was great among the nations!
> She that was a princess among the provinces
>   has become a vassal. (Lamentations 1.1)

Among all the sad verses in Lamentations is one concerning the king, here referred to as the 'anointed', being referred to as the one who exercised a crucial role in the national life, the God-appointed person who would guide and lead his people, and under whose wise and beneficent rule they would live in safety and security in the world of the nations:

> The Lord's anointed, the breath of our life.
>   was taken in their pits –
> the one of whom we said, 'Under his shadow
>   we shall live among the nations.'
> (Lamentations 4.20)

Of course, it did not always work out quite like that. The kings of
Israel and Judah were frequently not as good as that, and all too
often they failed their people, and often if there was a prophet
they were roundly condemned. Thus Jeremiah the prophet had –
at least as far as we are told – nothing good to say about
Jehoiakim the son of Josiah and at one time king in Jerusalem:

> They shall not lament for him, saying,
>   'Alas, my brother!' or 'Alas, sister!'
> They shall not lament for him, saying,
>   'Alas, lord!' or 'Alas, his majesty!'
> With the burial of a donkey he shall be buried –
>   dragged off and thrown out beyond the gates
>   of Jerusalem. (Jeremiah 22.18–19)

The prophet Isaiah never, as far as we are aware, had such a
harsh word to say about a king in Jerusalem. There are indeed
harsh words uttered in the book of Isaiah about the kings of
Assyria and Babylonia (10.12–19; 13.11; 37.22–29), and that
because of their arrogant and boastful pride. But that is another
matter, and for the present my concern is with the Jerusalemite
kings. Yet the prophet Isaiah of Jerusalem *is* critical of King Ahaz
of Judah in the setting of the attack upon Judah and Jerusalem by
a coalition of two small states, Israel under King Pekah and Syria
(Aram) under King Rezin. We read about this in the book of
Isaiah chapters 7 and 8, and also in 2 Kings 16, then in 2 Chronicles 28, and maybe also in Hosea 5.8 to 7.16.

Isaiah's complaint with Ahaz is not that he has behaved arro-
gantly with his people, or even that he has been incompetent in
the exercise of his kingship. It is quite simply that he has not been

the man of faith in God that he should have been. It is not, I
think that he should have been a person who just prayed to God
for himself and his people in this time of national crisis and then
have taken no particular action for their defence. My reading of
these particular chapters of the book suggests to me that the burden of the prophet's complaint with the king was that the king
lacked the basic foundation of religious faith in God, a foundation that should have been firm so that upon it, and in the light
of it, and in consequence of it, he could then make his political
calculations and military deployments. Thus the prophet was
commanded by God to say to the king:

> Take heed, be quiet, do not fear, and do not let your heart
> be faint because of these two smouldering stumps of fire-
> brands, because of the fierce anger of Rezin and Aram
> and the son of Remaliah....
>
> If you do not stand firm in faith,
>   you shall not stand at all. (Isaiah 7.4, 9b)

It would appear that this King Ahaz wearied the prophet Isaiah,
a weariness with the attitude of Ahaz that the prophet believed
he shared with God. For when the prophet invited the king to ask
for any sign from the Lord that might confirm him in his none-
too-steady or robust faith, Ahaz replied that he would not ask
such a thing of God, putting God to the test. Thus the prophet
responded, somewhat warmly it seems:

> Hear then, O house of David! Is it too little for you to
> weary mortals, that you weary my God also? Therefore
> the Lord himself will give you a sign. Look, the young
> woman is with child and shall bear a son, and shall call
> him Immanuel. (Isaiah 7.13–14)

This, of course, is the celebrated 'Immanuel Sign', and one can
only hope that its meaning was more obvious to its originally
intended recipient, King Ahaz, than it has been to Old
Testament scholars ever since. But my point is the general sense

of dissatisfaction that there was on the part of the prophet Isaiah with this particular king, Ahaz the son of Jotham.

One reaction that we might have expected as a result of this bad incident in the exercise of the responsibilities of Israelite kingship would have been to long for the day when there were human kings no more, or even to work for the elimination of kingship in Jerusalem. And I suggest that this should not be regarded as such an impossible or surprising possibility for the reason that when kingship was introduced into Israelite society it is clear to us that it was the cause of serious division of thought. Some of the stories in the books of Samuel witness to the fact that while there were those in Israel who believed that kingship would be a good thing, either because the united leadership of the nation was needed in the face of the the threat of the Philistines, or else because there were those who quite simply wished to be part of a nation that was more like the nations who were round about. And it seems that at various times in ancient Israel there were those who were unhappy about the institution of kingship, and about the power that kings might abrogate for themselves. For when all was said and done Israel believed itself to be a nation that lived under the kingship of God, and in the thought of some people acceptance and faithfulness to that divine king-ship did not make for an easy accomodation with a human king.

This emphasis, that Yahweh is the real king of Israel, is cer-tainly sounded in the book of Isaiah. It is there in the chapter about the overwhelming vision of the holiness and majesty of God that the prophet had in what appears to have been the temple in Jerusalem. The prophet says in tones of wonder:

> Woe is me! I am lost, for I am a man of unclean lips, and
> I live among a people of unclean lips; yet my eyes have
> seen the King, the Lord of hosts! (Isaiah 6.5)

And it is there in chapter 33, with its,

> For the Lord is our judge, the Lord is our ruler,
>   the Lord is our king; he will save us. (Isaiah 33.22)

And, in view of what I shall go on to say, we should take note of three references among the prophecies in chapters 40 to 55, each of which speaks of the kingship of God over his people:

> Set forth your case, says the Lord;
>> bring your proofs, says the King of Jacob.
> (Isaiah 41.21)

> I am the Lord, your Holy One,
>> the Creator of Israel, your King. (Isaiah 43.15)

> Thus says the Lord, the King of Israel,
>> and his Redeemer, the Lord of Hosts:
> I am the first and I am the last;
>> besides me there is no god. (Isaiah 44.6)

But to return to Isaiah of Jerusalem, and the incident of the Syro-Ephraimite war, an incident that showed up King Ahaz of Judah in such poor light. In fact the prophet Isaiah far from letting this incident drive him in the direction of abandoning thoughts about the institution of human Israelite kings, appears to have gone in completely the other direction. For while chapters 7 and 8 of the book of Isaiah treat the matter of the Syro-Ephraimite war, the following chapter, 9, contains a vision of an ideal king of the line of David who will one day rule with military success and with great wisdom. And though he will be a human king of the line of David, yet will he approach close to the realms of divinity. For here are some the Old Testament's boldest words about the greatness of an Israelite king:

> For a child has been born for us,
>> a son given to us;
> authority rests upon his shoulders;
>> and he is named
> Wonderful Counsellor, Mighty God,
>> Everlasting Father, Prince of Peace.
> His authority shall grow continually,
>> and there shall be endless peace

for the throne of David and his kingdom.
　　He will establish and uphold it
　with justice and with righteousness
　　　from this time onwards and for evermore.
The zeal of the Lord of hosts will do this. (Isaiah 9.6–7)

And these early chapters in the book of Isaiah have in 11.1–5 a
further hopeful – even glowing – vision of the ideal king who no
doubt in the imaginings of some people in ancient Israel would
one day come and rule over them.

What further references are there to Israelite and Judean kings
in the book of Isaiah? We hear a good deal of Hezekiah in the
bridging material between the Assyrian and Babylonian parts of
the book (chapters 36 to 39). These chapters are unlike anything
else in the book of Isaiah, largely being paralleled by 2 Kings
18.13—20.19, and though the matter is complex, in all probability the Isaiah chapters are dependant upon the Kings material.[1]
Nevertheless the references to Hezekiah in Isaiah 36 to 39 speak
about day-to-day matters rather than giving visions of future
human kings.

However there *are* two further references to kings in Isaiah 1 to
39 that we should note before we proceed, one unclear and other
clear. First the one that is not clear: and it is not clear in the sense
that it is difficult to know whether the talk in this verse is about
the heavenly king, or about an earthly one. It occurs in chapter
33, a chapter that displays a wide variety of themes and styles.[2]
At any rate, verse 17 reads:

Your eyes will see the king in his beauty;
　they will behold a land that stretches far away.
(Isaiah 33.17)

As I say, we cannot be sure whether the reference here is to the
divine or an earthly king. I incline to the view that it is the divine
king, and in this present context I shall not refer to this verse again.

But the other verse I am concerned about is clearer, and it is a
forward-looking verse, in which a prophet envisages a day when

there will be good, just and wise human kingship in Jerusalem, and when thus there will be safe and beneficent rule for his subject peoples. Thus:

> See, a king will rule in righteousness,
>   and princes will rule with justice.
> Each will be like a hiding place from the wind,
>   a covert from the tempest,
> like streams of water in a dry place,
>   like the shade of a great rock in a weary land.
> (Isaiah 32.1–2)

And that, at the beginning of chapter 32, is the last vision that we are given in the sixty-six-chapter book of Isaiah of a coming human king. Further, after Isaiah 39.3 – that is, at the close of those chapters about the goings-on of prophet and king in the days of Hezekiah – there is no mention of a Judean king. There are no more pictures in the book of Isaiah of a king who will reign in Jerusalem either in rightousness or otherwise. In chapters 40 to 55, with their glowing pictures and promises of the end of Babylonian exile and instead restored life in Jerusalem, there is no mention of a king who will rule in Jerusalem. And nor is there any mention of such a king in chapters 56 to 66, those chapters that appear to come from the years of re-establishment of national and religious life back home, centred on the holy city of Jerusalem. That is, in the book of Isaiah, by the time we have reached chapter 40, the Israelite king may be said to be dead.

Moreover, nor does there appear to be in the rest of the book of Isaiah any expectation, or even hope, that the kingship in Jerusalem, is going to be revived, resuscitated, resurrected, what have you. How are we to explain this? I wish to put forward various reasons that may account for the silence about the Israelite kingship in Isaiah 40 to 66.

In the first place we can say this. The historical era that we are speaking about is that of the Persian empire in the days of Cyrus, who entered Babylon in triumph in 539 BC, so completing his conquest of the Babylonian empire. Of course, in those preceding fifty or so years of the Babylonian empire that the people of Judah and Jerusalem had spent in exile in Babylon there was no way that they could have a king. They had lived under Babylonian rule, and that probably was the reason why the Babylonians had taken them away from their own homeland. Most likely in those long years of exile there was a considerable amount of work being done compiling documents, that would set out Israelite traditions, tell their religious and national histories, seeking to learn lessons from the past as to the relationship that should have existed in past times between these people and their God – and what levels of faithfulness must prevail in future times unless continued catastrophe was going to be the order of the day. Perhaps it was there in Babylon that the closing chapter of the books of Kings was composed, with what is maybe a hint of hope that there could be a future for the Jerusalemite kingship. This was when the king of Babylon,

> spoke kindly to him [Jehoiachin], and gave him a seat above the other seats of the kings who were with him in Babylon. So Jehoiachin put aside his prison clothes. Every day of his life he dined regularly in the king's presence. For his allowance, a regular allowance was given him by the king, a portion every day, as long as he lived. (2 Kings 25.28–30)

But that expression of hope, if indeed it was intended to be an expression of hope, was never to be realised. It would not happen while the Babylonian power prevailed, and then when the Persians gained the upper hand in the Mesopotamian lands it could not happen. For while Cyrus, that most enlightened Persian ruler might have allowed his subject peoples to return home to their own lands, and to have a certain degree of national and religious independence, being able among other things to worship their own gods, clearly he could not allow them to have their own kings. They were under the Persian rule, and that quite simply is the first reason we may give for this absence of any vision or hint in the later parts of the book of Isaiah about the possible rule of

a king in Jerusalem. The sheer reality of the political situation of
a people who were under the lordship of a mighty nation dictated
that there could be no thought of their having their own king.

There is secondly this to be said. While in Isaiah 40 to 55 –
chapters that speak in thrilling prophecies of the fast-approach-
ing day when the people of Judah and Jerusalem will be able to
go home – (and at that all along their specially and divinely prepared processional highway, and with divine protection both
before and after them [40.3–5; 49.8–13; 52.7–12]) – there is no
talk of any future Jerusalem king. In fact the human personality,
or personalities, occupying the dominating place in these chapters is the servant, or the servants. I am thinking about those four
passages that have been so-much discussed and studied, namely,
Isaiah 42.1–4; 49.1–6; 50.4–9, and 52.13—53.12. Many students
of these chapters believe that it is just one servant who is being
spoken about in these passages. My own view is that these are
four pictures of the life and the way of servanthood, pictures that,
I suggest, are intended to speak about aspects of the future life of
the people of Judah in Jerusalem in their re-established national
and religious life back in their old homeland.[3]

Now it has been argued in recent years that kingly traits have
been subsumed in these pictures of the servant, and that aspects
of the functions and the responsibilities of the king are to be
taken up in the work of the servant.[4] But I think that it goes
deeper than that, and that instead of hearing about the king we
now read about the servant. I see this as a great insight that a
prophet of Israel was given as a result of his people's experience
of loss of national independence, through their having to live in
a new way in the world of the nations, and having indeed to
endure suffering, all these in the years of Babylonian exile. It is an
insight that perhaps could hardly have been given until that time
and experience. While they were an independent – or reasonably
independent – nation living in their own land, then Israelite
people could have a king who would lead them into battle and
secure their life and their borders against their enemies. Such in
past times was their style of life, and such must have seemed to be

a style of life that was consonant with their exalted status as God's people, God's chosen people.

But that style of life and national independence came to an end with the fall of Jerusalem to the Babylonians and the destruction of the temple in 587 BC. That searing experience must have given rise to much thinking and heart searching on the part of the people of Judah and Jerusalem in their time in exile, and particularly so on the part of their theologians. And I wish to suggest that one of the great insights granted to the exilic prophet of Isaiah 40 to 55 was that in future days there would not be a king, but instead there would a servant people. Surely this prophet was thinking more deeply than merely accepting that because of the political reality of the situation kingship was out and servanthood was in. It was a matter of coming to a sense of the presence of God in their situation of powerlessness, and I suggest that it was an insight also about the 'powerlessness' of God in his ways with his people. For while these chapters 40 to 55 of Isaiah may speak in such exalted tones of the one God who is the mighty Lord of all things and beings – of the stars in the heaven as well as of all the people of earth (48.12–16) – yet it also speaks in a sense of God's 'failure' with his people, a 'failure' with them that had been due to his having left them free, allowing them to have been spiritually deaf and blind servants (43.8) to his ways. In order to enable that relationship of human freedom to prevail, the mighty Lord of all – who according to the prophet of Isaiah 40 to 55 knows the names of all the stars in heaven (40.26) – has to be 'powerless' with his people, in the sense that they are free to follow his will or go in their own way, trust in him or trust in some other being, divine or human. Israel in exile in Babylon began to learn in its own experience this sense of powerlessness.

Yet it is surely even more than that. It is a matter of these people having come to their new insights through the experience of suffering, an insight that would not have come to them apart from the experience of exilic life, from having been forcibly deported from their homeland by a foreign power. We can see how Israel quite simply came to understand that most uncomfortable fact of life, that we each have to come to understand, that it is in the times of our sufferings and setbacks that we come to our greatest insights into God and his ways with us. Moreover, it is in those very times that we grow the most in our religious faith and understanding.

I wish to suggest that there were three great insights that were given through the experience of the exile to the individual who was responsible for the four passages about servanthood found in Isaiah 40 to 55. These three insights are reflected in what that prophet sets forth in the servant passages.

The first insight concerns the nations, in particular that in future days the people of Israel will have a mission to those nations. Whereas in the past, Israel might have acknowledged the lordship of Yahweh over the foreign nations, and if the witness of some the prophets' Oracles against the Nations are to be believed, may have expected those nations to obey Yahweh's laws (for example Amos 1.3—2.3), yet even so in those pre-exilic times did not feel any particular call or compulsion to proclaim the rule of Yahweh to those peoples.

However, in the first passage about a servant, the call is to an individual to 'bring forth justice to the nations' (42.1), and the meaning of the word 'justice' here is perhaps something akin to 'true religion', that is, Yahweh religion. In this passage it is stressed that this servant will persevere in his task of proclaiming Yahwistic religion to the peoples of the earth, and we are told that there are some areas of the world actively awaiting his coming:

> He will not grow faint or be crushed
>> until he has established justice in the earth;
>> and the coastlands wait for his teaching. (Isaiah 42.4)

And it is there too in the second of the servant passages (49.1–6), which opens with the servant addressing coastlands, 'peoples from far away' (49.1). The Lord is spoken of in this passage as calling the servant from what is in comparison the rather minor task of a ministry among the people of Israel and instead to go to a far wider constituency:

He [the Lord] says,
'It is too light a thing that you should be my servant
    to raise up the tribes of Jacob
    and to restore the survivors of Israel;
I will give you as a light to the nations,
    that my salvation may reach to the end of the earth.'
(Isaiah 49.6)

That was surely an insight that came out of the experience of God's people having to live away from their homeland, having to rub shoulders with the nations, having to find the presence and the purposes of God in a strange land.

The second new insight that we find in the passages about the servant is to be found in the third passage (50.4–9), and concerns suffering. The mission of this servant is in no way going to have a triumphalistic or victorious aspect to it. Indeed, the servant will suffer in the process of faithfully fulfilling his God-given mission. Here it is the servant who speaks:

I gave my back to those who struck me,
    and my cheeks to those who pulled out the beard;
I did not hide my face
    from insult and spitting. (Isaiah 50.6)

And we can surely understand that that also was an insight that came out of Israel's time of exile in Babylon, no longer being able to control their own national affairs, having perforce to live in servitude to others.

And the third new insight, and no doubt the greatest, concerns the fact that the sufferings at present being borne by an individual or a people may be used positively in the purposes of God, even redemptively. That is, through the sufferings of one, good things may happen for another. This, I think, is an insight that the individual responsible for the fourth of the servant passages (52.13—53.12) saw in a rather faltering way, something he saw as if through a glass darkly. This, of course is not in the least surprising, for this, as far as we can tell, was a completely new insight, something without parallel at the time, and that is not repeated in any later document that came to be included in the Old Testament.

This insight is expressed by those who witness the sufferings, and even the death, of one person, and 'they' come to see that the sufferings that 'they' should have borne have been taken by 'him', and that in 'his' sufferings there is healing for 'them':

> Surely he has borne our infirmities
>   and carried our diseases;
> yet we accounted him stricken,
>   struck down by God, and afflicted.
> But he was wounded for our transgressions,
>   crushed for our iniquities;
> upon him was the punishment that made us whole,
>   and by his bruises we are healed.
> All we like sheep have gone astray;
>   we have all turned to our own way,
> and the Lord has laid on him
>   the iniquity of us all. (Isaiah 53.4–6)

Many Christians see here a clear and unambiguous reference to the life, death and resurrection of Jesus. My own view is that we should understand the passage as having a primary focus on individuals and communities who lived at the time that this prophecy seems to come from, than those of some five centuries later. But undoubtedly, it is more than reasonable that Christians understand that this insight finds its ultimate fulfilment in Jesus. Whatever view one takes as to the individual spoken about here, and his ministry, the radical thoughts being set forth here do reflect the way that things would in fact go in the fulness of time for God's people.

It is clear that one of the deep problems that Jesus faced in his relationship with his disciples was to make them understand and accept that if he was to fulfil his God-given mission he would be rejected by the very people whose release he had come to secure, that he would have to suffer, and even to die. About these matters the disciples were incredulous, and their spokesman Simon Peter sought to dissuade Jesus in his determination to take this course (see for example Mark 8.31–33; 9.30–32; 10.32–34). Further, as we know, it was not just Jesus who was called to take this way, but that there were aspects of suffering that his followers were warned would come their way too, as they were faithful in their discipleship of Christ. Thus we read that Jesus

> called the crowd with his disciples, and said to them, 'If any want to become my followers, let them deny themselves and take up their cross and follow me.' (Mark 8.34)

Even more starkly, in Luke's Gospel there comes the warning that this taking up the cross, the embracing of this manner and style of discipleship, is something that has to be done *daily*:

> Then he [Jesus] said to them all, 'If any want to become my followers, let them deny themselves and take up their cross daily and follow me.' (Luke 9.23)

And it seems that there was that strand of thought in the early Christian Church that emphasised that it was only through the way of suffering that disciples would be truly and fully faithful to their Lord. Thus we read in the letter to the Colossians:

> I am now rejoicing in my sufferings for your sake, and in my flesh I am completing what is lacking in Christ's afflictions for the sake of his body, that is, the church. (Colossians 1.24)

If my understanding about the parts of the book of Isaiah that I have been speaking about is correct, and in particular that the four passages about the servant are in fact about aspects of how the future work of God's people will be done, then truly in the providential guidance of God the way was prepared, and God's people were forwarned. For as it was in the book of Isaiah, so did it become for both Christ and his disciples, and no doubt it ever will be for the followers of Christ in all the ages to come, that 'The King is Dead! Long Live the Servant!'

II

ISAIAH AND THE

SPIRITUAL SEARCH

'Spirituality', as I understand it, is about 'the way we are with God',[5] about 'the personal relation of people with God'.[6] That is, spirituality is about 'living', something more than 'believing', for spirituality is more than theology, the formulation of our beliefs about God and his relationships with the world and its people. It has been said that, 'Christian spirituality is not simply for "the interior life" or the inward person, but as much for the body as the soul, and is directed to the implementation of both the commandments of Christ, to love God and our neighbour.'[7]

Like many contemporary Christians I am interested in spirituality, in fact more than interested for I am concerned to discover a Christian spirituality for myself that is both faithful to the historic faith into which I am privileged to enter, and is appropriate to the age and setting in which I live. Can we find a Christian 'way with God' for our lives today?

The contributory sources that go into the fashioning of a Christian spirituality are many and varied. Apart from the witness of many Christian lives, both past and present, there are the traditions of the various parts of the Church, and, naturally, there is all that is contributed through the biblical material. In this last-named the New Testament clearly has a pre-eminent contribution to make, but surely also the Old Testament, for *pace* Marcion and all his (conscious or unconscious) modern proponents, this is a part of the Christian canon of Scripture.[8] Thus I ask myself what might be the particular contributions that the Old Testament makes to our spiritual search today. However, to

127

deal with the whole of the Old Testament in this regard is a major undertaking, so for the present I content myself by asking what might be the contribution that the book of Isaiah makes to our spirituality? [9]

Naturally, the objection may be made that it is not legitimate to ask of an ancient work a question that springs from the concerns of a much later, and vastly different, age. Yet, the book of Isaiah is part of Christian scripture, a fact that carries with it both the promise and the conviction that it does have something to contribute to our Christian lives today. Moreover, while the concerns of Christian people in the twenty-first century about, say, genetic engineering or medical ethics may be of a totally different order to the questions and concerns being addressed in the Isaiah book, yet in the matter of spirituality there is surely a marked sense of continuity, even déjà vu. For though the language and expression may be different, still the underlying subject and concern is the same. Spirituality is in the first place concerned with the relationship between individuals or communities and God, and this is the very subject with which the book opens.

The first chapter of the book of Isaiah has been widely regarded – and rightly in my judgement – as intended to serve as introduction to what follows. In it are outlined some of the main themes that will be expanded upon, illustrated, fleshed-out, in the contents of the following chapters. Yet the fundamental problem that is being probed in the first part of the book (chapters 1 to 39) is that God's people have failed in their relationship with him: no longer do they have regard for him; they no longer 'know' him, that is, 'have a relationship' with him. Thus:

> The ox knows its owner,
>   and the donkey its master's crib;
> but Israel does not know,
>   my people do not understand. (Isaiah 1.3)

It is as if to say, in the language of the western twenty-first century Christian Church, that the spiritual search of these people is no longer taking place. The place of God – or at least the place of Yahweh, the God of Israel – in their lives is no longer a matter of serious concern, consideration or search on the part of these people.

This concern about the failure of the Israelite people in their relationship with God will be teased out, given expression, and expanded upon in a wide range of situations and historical settings. It is there, for example, in the crisis for Judah and Jerusalem when they were attacked by a (in fact, weak) coalition of states, Israel and Syria (Isaiah 7 and 8). In that setting, so the prophet Isaiah proclaims, the essential foundation for any decision, any action, must be faith and trust in God, and that it is these qualities that are conspicuous by their absence, at least on the part of Ahaz, the king. Thus the prophet's word from the Lord to Ahaz in Isaiah 7.9b was about standing 'firm in faith', even though in the moment of crisis the power of God may give the appearance of being strangely small (Isaiah 8.6).

At a much later stage in the book the point is made that without a deep faith and trust in God there will be no future life for the people, and that without this faith and trust the Lord will not be able to continue to work out his purposes through them. In particular, it is only as the exiles' faith in God is rekindled will they find within them the necessary trust in God, so necessary as they go out on their perilous journey through the wilderness, what was truly – as we might say – a step in faith. Thus the prophet of chapters 40 to 55 begins by saying how great God is (40.12–26), and goes on to assert that in trust in the Lord is sufficient strength for each stage of life's journey:

> Even youths will faint and be weary,
>   and the young will fall exhausted;
> but those who wait for the Lord shall renew
>   their strength,
>   they shall mount up with wings like eagles,
> they shall run and not be weary,
>   they shall walk and not faint.
> (Isaiah 40.30–31)

But spirituality, as I have argued is about even more than the relationship between human beings and God, but is also about the whole of the way that human beings lead their lives. That is, spirituality is also about the relationship between believers and their neighbours. And it is clear that what is being portrayed in the opening chapter of the Isaiah book is a situation in which all of those relationships – both those between people and God and those between people and people – have gone haywire. Thus as regards the relationships of neighbour with neighbour the prophet thunders:

> How the faithful city
>   has become a whore!
>   She that was full of justice,
> righteousness lodged in her –
>   but now murderers!
> Your silver has become dross,
>   your wine is mixed with water.
> Your princes are rebels
>   and companions of thieves.
> Everyone loves a bribe
>   and runs after gifts.
> They do not defend the orphan,
>   and the widow's cause does not come before them.
> (Isaiah 1.21–23)

And later:

> For the vineyard of the Lord of hosts
>   is the house of Israel,
> and the people of Judah
>   are his pleasant planting;
> he expected justice,
>   but saw bloodshed;
> righteousness,
>   but heard a cry!
> (Isaiah 5.7)

Enough has been said to make the point that the early chapters of the book of Isaiah portray situations in which a desirable and appropriate spirituality on the part of the people of Israel is conspicuous only by its absence. Their relationships have all broken down; their spirituality is broken up. What then, we may ask, does this book have to contribute of a positive nature regarding a desirable order of spirituality on the part of Israel? How is this Humpty Dumpty envisaged as being put together again? What indeed is there set forth in this book whereby the broken fragments of a spirituality may be put together, or even fashioned into a new vessel?

The Old Testament is made up of a remarkably varied collection of materials coming from a wide range of settings and perhaps intended for another wide range of settings and situations. Even single books within the whole present similar difficulties, the book of Isaiah certainly being no exception. For here is no systematic treatment of a set of themes and ideas, but something much more in the nature of a collection of materials that come from different historical eras and a wide range of situations. How then may one organise and categorise this material as regards spirituality? I suggest that in this case of the book of Isaiah one may usefully consider four 'dimensions' of spirituality towards which the contents of the book point us: (1) the exaltation of the Lord; (2) the wide and all-embracing nature of his rule and authority; (3) the vast sweep of the historical process that he embraces; and (4) the call to humility and trust in him on the part of the people of earth. That is, there is emphasised here in this book aspects of the height, breadth, length and depth of the things of God (compare Ephesians 3.18), and to these I now turn.

(1) First I consider height, that is that marked emphasis in the book concerning the 'otherness' of the Lord, his exaltation, the lofty elevation of his supposed dwelling place. Even when in his earthly setting the prophet Isaiah has a vision of this God, the Lord's throne is regarded as elevating him to a place 'high and lofty' (6.1). The third part of the book speaks too of the lofty elevation both of the Lord and of his dwelling place:

> For thus says the high and lofty one
>   who inhabits eternity, whose name is Holy:
> I dwell in the high and holy place ... (Isaiah 57.15)

Something of this greatness and exaltation of Yahweh is spoken about in chapter 40 in the oracles with which the prophecies of the so-called Second Isaiah begin:

> Who has measured the waters in the hollow of his hand
>   and marked off the heavens with a span,
> enclosed the dust of the earth in a measure,
>   and weighed the mountains in scales
>   and the hills in a balance? (Isaiah 40.12)

This, of course, is one of the oft-recurring rhetorical questions, a characteristic feature of this part of the book, and intended to draw forth the obvious – in fact, the only possible – answer namely that it is none other than the Lord God. He alone is the creator of the world (see 40.12–26, especially verse 26; also 48.13 and 51.16).

In Isaiah's inaugural vision, 'holy' is the word on the lips of the seraphim as they utter their praises of the Lord:

> Holy, holy, holy is the Lord of hosts;
>   the whole earth is full of his glory. (Isaiah 6.3)

While this word (Hebrew *qādōsh*) connotes primarily distance, otherness, separateness, the element of 'purity' is not totally lacking.[10] Isaiah 5.16 speaks of the exaltation and separateness of Yahweh being made particularly evident in his acting in righteousness and justice:

> But the Lord of hosts is exalted by justice,
>   and the Holy God shows himself holy by
>   righteousness. (Isaiah 5.16)

Thus it is no light matter for any human individual to be confronted by the greatness and majesty, the holiness and otherness of this Lord God. This is made particularly clear in the account of the prophet's vision of the Holy One in 6.1–8, a vision that at one and the same time highlights divine otherness and human sinfulness:

> And I said: 'Woe is me! I am lost, for I am a man of un-
> clean lips, and I live among a people of unclean lips; yet
> my eyes have seen the King, the Lord of hosts!' (Isaiah 6.5)

Here there is emphasised the great distance, gulf one might say, between the deity and the people of earth. There is thus a sense of wonder that this mighty God should have a care for his people. Yet in chapter 40 the Second Isaiah having spoken of the mighty creating and preserving activity of God (40.12–26), goes on to speak of his relationship with and care for his chosen people:

> Why do you say, O Jacob,
>   and speak, O Israel,
> 'My way is hidden from the Lord,
>   and my right is disregarded by my God'?
> (Isaiah 40.27)

Rather:

> But those who wait for the Lord shall renew their
>   strength,
>   they shall mount up with wings like eagles,
> they shall run and not be weary,
>   they shall walk and not faint. (Isaiah 40.31)

But – and this is surely the crucial point – the one with whom these people have this relationship is none other than the sovereign Lord, the creator and maker of all (40.22; 42.5; 43.1), the first and the last, besides whom there is no other (41.4; 44.6; 48.12). He may be the Holy One of Israel (1.4; 5.19, 24 and elsewhere), but Israel must never forget that he is above all the Holy One.

All this is to say that the first aspect of a spirituality having any dependence on the book of Isaiah must be this emphasis on the exaltation and otherness of the Lord. It is that sense of the numinous, that root aspect of religion, the apprehension of the

mysterium tremendum et fascinans that Rudolph Otto probed so per-
ceptively in his important study of many years ago, *The Idea of
the Holy*. And indeed, Otto himself in that work not infrequently
makes reference to the book of Isaiah, in one place observing, 'If
a man does not *feel* [his italics] what the numinous is, when he
reads the sixth chapter of Isaiah, then no "preaching, singing,
telling", in Luther's phrase, can avail him.' [11]

(2) Then the second 'dimension' of spirituality in the book of
Isaiah to which I suggest we should attend is all that emphasis
found here on the wide and all-embracing sphere of activity of
the Lord. There is a particular 'breadth' to this that is here given
marked expression. In some parts of the book this emphasis is
found in ways we already know from our reading of other Old
Testament prophetic collections. For, while we have a collection
of oracles against various nations in Isaiah 13 to 23, so also do we
in Amos (1.3 to 2.3), in Jeremiah (46 to 51), and in Ezekiel (25 to
32). And while we cannot claim to understand the full import of
the presence of these 'nation oracles' in the prophetic books,
what is clear is that they point to serious belief in the reality of the
Lord's rule not merely within the boundaries of the lands of
Israel and Judah, but also over a much wider, vaster territory.

Thus far there are few surprises. But this is not all. For here in
Isaiah is the vision – also to be found in Micah 4.1–4, and it is not
clear to us which of these versions is the 'original', or whether in
fact in both settings they are drawn from a common earlier version.

> Many peoples shall come and say,
> 'Come, let us go up to the mountain of the Lord,
>   to the house of the God of Jacob;
> that he may teach us his ways
>   and that we may walk in his paths.'
> For out of Zion shall go forth instruction,
>   and the word of the Lord from Jerusalem.
> (Isaiah 2.3)

Then again, in the prophet's inaugural vision in the temple the
cry of the seraphim concerned not only the holiness of the Lord,

but also carried the assertion that the whole earth is full of the divine glory (that is, what there is in the transcendent divine holiness that can be revealed on earth):

> Holy, holy, holy is the Lord of hosts;
> the whole earth is full of his glory. (Isaiah 6.3)

In the prophecies of the Second Isaiah we read that when the mighty events of the new exodus of the people of Israel take place:

> Then the glory of the Lord shall be revealed,
>   and all people shall see it together,
>   for the mouth of the Lord has spoken.
> (Isaiah 40.5; see also 52.10)

This is the God who in order to fulfil his chosen purposes can work his mighty works through the human agency of the Persian ruler Cyrus, as indeed earlier he had worked through the Assyrian ruler (10.5–6):

> Who says of Cyrus, 'He is my shepherd,
>   and he shall carry out all my purpose'.
> (Isaiah 44.28a)

Indeed, for Second Isaiah this is the God of the whole earth (54.5), and earlier in the book is a remarkable oracle (most likely dating from post-exilic times) that speaks of nations who more than witnessing the glory of the Lord, actively worship him. Thus:

> On that day there will be a highway from Egypt to Assyria, and the Assyrian will come into Egypt, and the Egyptian into Assyria, and the Egyptians will worship with the Assyrians. On that day Israel will be the third with Egypt and Assyria, a blessing in the midst of the earth, whom the Lord of hosts has blessed, saying, 'Blessed be Egypt my people, and Assyria the work of my hands, and Israel my heritage.' (Isaiah 19.23–25)

This truly is a remarkable passage in its confident affirmation of the Lord's sovereignty over many peoples. Here, the Lord, 'claims

them as his own possession and puts them into the stream of blessings, which had been made visible to Israel at first, but which now
would spread out over the "heathen" as well. One is not far from
Paul's "to the Jew first and also to the Greek" (Romans 1.16).' [12]

In a rather less grandiose way the Second Isaiah envisages a
day when various foreign people would join themselves to Jewish
people (for example 44.5), and it is clear that when something of
that did actually begin to take place in the post-exilic community,
it raised a wide range of issues that hitherto had hardly been considered, much less confronted. Thus, for example, Ezra 4.1-3 represents a less than wholeheartedly welcoming view, what we
might call a strict approach to Israelite national purity. In contrast, the third part of the Isaiah book (chapters 56 to 66) displays
a much more open and welcoming approach to such peoples, and
speaks of them having a place in the worship life in the renewed
Jerusalem (see Isaiah 56.7–8).

There is thus in the book of Isaiah what I have called this
marked element of breadth. Here is both warning and challenge
to God's people that they must ever be prepared for change as the
perceived domain of God increases and broadens. Although this
book may make considerable use of that divine title 'Holy One of
Israel' it behoves us to take serious note of the fact that the tendency of the whole work is towards the expression of the fact that
the Lord is the Holy One of all peoples. Its near-closing word
concerns the vision of all flesh coming to worship before the Lord
(66.23). That is to say, any spirituality that takes this book with
any seriousness must pay attention to this inclusiveness, this
emphasis on the wide and all-embracing nature of the Lord's rule
and authority.

(3) Then third, 'length', by which I mean the vast sweep of the
historical process that the Lord embraces. That is, there is a vast
length of historical time encompassed in the 'story' being 'told'
here of God's people, his judgement upon them, his forgiveness
and restoration of them, of their relationships with other peoples
and authorities in the world.

We have become accustomed to speak of the three main parts

of the Isaiah book as the Assyrian (chapters 1 to 39), the Babylonian (chapters 40 to 55), and the Persian (chapters 56 to 66). That is, the whole book encompasses a great span of historical eras, of times that begin with the days of Israel's political independence in the lands of Judah and Israel in whose capital cities there ruled respectively the Judean and Israelite kings. Yet lowering over these settings was already the growing might of Assyria. And while the king of Assyria may have successfully conquered Israel and Samaria, even he had to acknowledge defeat as far as Jerusalem was concerned (chapters 36 to 37).

Yet what the Assyrian could not do, was successfully accomplished by the Babylonians, as a result of which there ensued close on half a century of exile in Babylon for the people of Judah and Jerusalem, painful years, and yet years burgeoning with growing insights and deepening theological approaches. The book, moreover, goes on to tell of the new possibilities initiated as a result of the conquest of Babylon by the Persian ruler Cyrus, in particular those occasioned by the novel approach of the Persians as regards the religious worship and place of residence of their subject peoples. Thus there opened up the thrilling, and yet at the same time challenging, possibilities of the exiles being able to worship their own God freely in their homeland.

Thus the Isaiah book speaks truly about a pilgrim people, about a people who live first in the homeland, who are then away in Babylon, and who later return home. But home is now different, and there are others too who come and join in. Truly, living – as it is portrayed here – is to change. Changes there are here, changes that teach new duties, and afford new insights. Yet towering over all this historical process is the Lord, the Holy One, who is indeed portrayed in the book of Isaiah as the Lord of history. A spirituality that builds on the insights of the book of Isaiah will surely have to take with seriousness this insight that at all times God's people are on pilgrimage. They, or their ancestors, have been led from one place and setting, both alike redolent with memories and insights into the life of faith, and they are being led on the way to new settings, places, insights. And all the while they

are being called and challenged to see the hand of God at work
in all this change and historical purpose. It is this:

> I am about to do a new thing;
>> now it springs forth, do you not perceive it?
> (Isaiah 43.19a)

> See, the former things have come to pass,
>> and new things I now declare.
> (Isaiah 42.9a)

(4) Then fourth, my category of 'depth' – by which I intend to
indicate those inner dimensions of faith in the Holy One to which
the people of God are continually being called in this book, the
call to the life of earthly humility and quiet yet strong trust in the
Lord. But there is also the call here to profound depths in the
spiritual life, unparalleled elsewhere in the pages of the Old
Testament.

If there is one particular aspect of the relationship between
people and God that is emphasised by Isaiah of Jerusalem it is
that of 'trust'. It is there, as we have already seen in the call of the
prophet to his king in the setting of the Syro-Ephraimite war
(Isaiah 7.9b), for the real sin of these people in the eyes of this
prophet is their profound lack of trust in God (Isaiah 8.6). The
real life for God's people – and for all manner of people so it says
in this book – lies in their turning to the Lord:

> Turn to me and be saved,
>> all the ends of the earth! (Isaiah 45.22a)

And then, the manner of life that is called for is one of humility
before the greatness of the Lord:

> For thus says the high and lofty one
>> who inhabits eternity, whose name is Holy:
> I dwell in the high and holy place,
>> and also with those who are contrite and
>>> humble in spirit,

> to revive the spirit of the humble,
>> and to revive the heart of the contrite. (Isaiah 57.15)

In order to capture the real force of this, it should be read alongside the condemnation expressed in those early chapters of the book where we hear of those who are proud, puffed up, and arrogant (see especially 2.9–22; 3.16–26; 5.14–15). But the *humble* style of life will surely lead naturally to a sense of true and profound worship of the Lord on the part of these people. Such dimensions of true worship are spoken about in 56.9—57.13 and in 58.1–14. But they are also to be observed in those hymns of praise that occur with some frequency throughout the Isaiah book, but especially so in chapters 40 to 55. See 12.1–6; 42.10–13; 44.23; 45.18; 49.13. And we should also note perhaps those passages in which Lord praises himself: 41.4b; 42.8; 43.10–13; 44.24–28; 45.6–7; 48.12–13; 51.15.

Meanwhile the people of earth being called to look to God in faith and in trust, are also called to a life of humility not only before God, but also before their neighbours. Right at the beginning of the book the themes of justice and righteousness, of the call to live the moral life, is emphasised.

> Wash yourselves; make yourselves clean;
>> remove the evil of your doings
>> from before my eyes;
> cease to do evil,
>> learn to do good;
> seek justice,
>> rescue the oppressed,
> defend the orphan,
>> plead for the widow. (Isaiah 1.16–17)

There are even more demanding things to come, in particular in the second part of the book where we read of the call to lives of service that will involve God's people in yet deeper commitment to the Lord's purposes, and also to depths of suffering not spoken about anywhere else in the Old Testament in quite such terms as here and with such force. I am referring, of course, to those four passages about a servant, or servants, that are found in chapters 40 to 55, namely 42.1–4; 49.1–6; 50.4–9 and 52.13—53.12. We do not need to go into any great detail about these passages here.[13] It seems to me that in these passages we are being presented with four pictures about new depths and aspects of the commitment and servanthood to which the people of Israel in post-exilic times will be called.

This, in the first place, will involve them in living lives of service for others. There will be the call to a new ministry of serving those who at present are beyond the bounds of the Israelite community. This is brought out in the first two of the passages about the 'servant' (42.1–4; 49.1–6). This must have been an insight that was gained by the prophet from the experience of having lived the years of exile in Babylon, and is a counterpart to that insight that the rule and purposes of the Lord have a great 'breadth', that is, they extend over a wide and far-flung geographical area. And as the Lord was understood in the closing years of the exile to be calling people from a wide range of lands, countries and political situations to become, along with his ancient people, those who acknowledged him as Lord (43.5–7; 49.12), so as a counterpart to this are God's people now called to go out to the nations to proclaim this Lord and his purposes. Thus of the servant – who surely represents Israel – it is said:

> He will not grow faint or be crushed
>   until he has established justice in the earth;
>   and the coastlands wait for his teaching. (Isaiah 42.4)

Christians, as they read this part of the book of Isaiah, can hardly fail to associate these words with those of the writer of the letter to the Ephesians:

> So he came and proclaimed peace to you who were far off
> and peace to those who were near; for through him both
> of us have access in one Spirit to the Father. So then you
> are no longer strangers and aliens, but you are citizens

with the saints and also members of the household of
God. (Ephesians 2.17–19)

or with the closing words of the Gospel according to Matthew:

Go therefore and make disciples of all nations, baptising
them in the name of the Father and of the Son and of the
Holy Spirit, and teaching them to obey everything that I
have commanded you. And remember, I am with you
always, to the end of the age. (Matthew 28.19–20)

But there are yet greater demands to be made upon this servant
people, for more than going out in the name of the Lord to other
peoples, they must also be ready to accept and embrace suffering
(50.4–9) and even sacrificial death that others may thereby have
life (52.13—53.12). It is as if this theme is introduced in comparatively gentle ways with the note of warning to the reader and
the hearer conveyed through the experience of the servant as
expressed in the third passage about the servant:

The Lord God has opened my ear,
    and I was not rebellious,
    I did not turn backwards.
I gave my back to those who struck me,
    and my cheeks to those who pulled out the beard;
I did not hide my face
    from insult and spitting.
(Isaiah 50.5–6)

But there is no gentleness, and little by way of comfort, in what is
said about the servant in the fourth of these passages. Here is the
witness of the unknown group who observe what is happening to
this servant:

He was despised and rejected by others;
    a man of suffering and acquainted with infirmity;
and as one from whom others hide their faces
    he was despised, and we held him of no account.

Surely he has borne our infirmities
    and carried our diseases;
yet we accounted him stricken,
    struck down by God, and afflicted.
But he was wounded for our transgressions,
    crushed for our iniquities;
upon him was the punishment that made us whole,
    and by his bruises we are healed.
(Isaiah 53.3–5)

And Christians as they read and hear this can hardly fail to be receiving, as if by some process of echo, those words of Jesus to his would-be followers:

If any want to become my followers, let them deny themselves and take up their cross daily and follow me. For those who want to save their life will lose it, and those who lose their life for my sake will save it. (Luke 9.23–24)

So in this way will love of God and commitment to him involve these people in whole new depths of love of their neighbours, and this alongside a deep and caring commitment to them. And it will be through such lives that a person's true happiness and reward will be found. Through such a manner of living, through such a lifestyle, will that person receive the coveted portion with the great:

Therefore I will allot him a portion with the great,
    and he shall divide the spoil with the strong;
because he poured out himself to death,
    and was numbered with the transgressors;
yet he bore the sin of many,
    and made intercession for the transgressors.
(Isaiah 53.12)

In these sorts of ways I suggest the book of Isaiah indicates to us some dimensions – lengths, breadths, heights and depths – for the spiritual life. Yet first there must be the appreciation that in this

Lord is to be found the real strength, meaning and purpose for a person's life:

> Surely God is my salvation;
>> I will trust, and will not be afraid,
> for the Lord God is my strength and my might;
>> he has become my salvation. (Isaiah 12.2)

And that will lead to a spirit of thankfulness and praise:

> Give thanks to the Lord,
>> call on his name;
> make known his deeds among the nations;
>> proclaim that his name is exalted.
> Sing praises to the Lord, for he has done gloriously;
>> let this be known in all the earth.
> Shout aloud and sing for joy, O royal Zion,
>> for great in your midst is the Holy One of Israel.
> (Isaiah 12.4–6)

And thus there comes the eternal call to commitment:

> O house of Jacob,
>> come, let us walk
>> in the light of the Lord! (Isaiah 2.5)

Yes, as we have seen, how much there is in the book of Isaiah to inform our Christian spirituality!

III

THE HOLY CITY:

JERUSALEM IN THE BOOK OF ISAIAH

What is it that is so special about Jerusalem? Karen Armstrong in her book about the history of Jerusalem tells us how both her Israeli and Palestinian guides to the city pointed out to her that Jerusalem is 'holy to their people'.[14] What can we say – attempting to paint a much more modest canvas than Karen Armstrong's – about the specialness of Jerusalem in the book of Isaiah? I will go about this in three sections. First, there are historical matters, then in the second place the portrayal of Jerusalem in the Isaiah book, and thirdly I will offer some reflections.

Matters historical

Until the time of the kingship of David (c.1000–961 BC) Jerusalem was a Jebusite city, in whose environs Israelite people felt no sense of security and peace after dark (Judges 19.10–12). David, having first become king of Judah in Hebron (2 Samuel 2.1–4), and then king of the Israelite tribes – yet still in Hebron (2 Samuel 5.1–3) – conquered Jerusalem with his own men and thus made it his own possession (2 Samuel 5.6–10). So Jerusalem became the city of David, and from that time onwards became increasingly established as the capital city of the Judean and Israelite tribes. Later, in the period of David's son Solomon's kingship, considerable building works took place in Jerusalem, none more significant than the construction of a temple on Mount Zion. We read about this in 1 Kings 5 to 8 and 2 Chronicles 3 to 4, and though we seem to be given here masses of information, yet many of the details given are not clear to us.

In the days of King Hezekiah (715–687 BC) the Assyrian king Sennacherib laid siege to Jerusalem, a matter that we read about in 2 Kings 18.13—19.37; Isaiah 36.1—37.38 and 2 Chronicles 32.1–23, and although the matter may appear in at least parts of these accounts to have been something of a close-run thing – the Assyrians being encamped just outside the city walls even so Jerusalem was spared and the Assyrians returned home. We read in what appears to have been one of a series of accounts that have become conflated in this material, that 'the angel of the Lord went forth and slew a hundred and eighty five thousand in the camp of the Assyrians' (2 Kings 19.35), and that the hostile army departed.

Then in 598 BC the Babylonians laid siege to the city, and unlike the Assyrians they were successful and they took captives, deporting them to Babylon (2 Kings 24.10–12). Yet still the city stood, but in that form not for long, for in 587 BC the Babylonians returned. They destroyed the temple, taking its treasures to Babylon as captured booty, and marching many of the people off into exile there. Others fled into exile elsewhere. Something of the deeply felt tragedy of these terrible events is recorded for us in the book of Lamentations.

> How lonely sits the city
> > that once was full of people!
> How like a widow she has become,
> > she that was great among the nations!
> She that was a princess among the provinces
> > has become a vassal. (Lamentations 1.1)

This distress did not last for ever, for in 539 BC the Persian conqueror of Babylon, Cyrus, allowed the exiled Jews in that city to return to their own land. In what is portrayed as something of a triumphal procession they made the journey back home to Jerusalem, taking with them the temple vessels that earlier had been carried away by Nebuchadnezzar along with his captives to Babylon (Ezra 1.7–11; 6.1–12). The rebuilding of Jerusalem began, Nehemiah apparently being one of the driving forces in this, and thus was a new temple built, this being completed in 515 BC under the leadership of Zerubbabel (Ezra 6.13–18). We are not given a description of this temple in the Old Testament, though we hear plenty about its priestly, levitical and other attendants, and its sacrifices (Ezra 2.36–54; 7.11–20; Nehemiah 10.32–39). Yet it could well be this temple that is being described, perhaps in rather idealistic light, by Aristeas in his letter to his brother Philocrates. In all probability Aristeas was an Egyptian Jew who wrote sometime between 250 and 100 BC.[15] What is without doubt is the enthusiasm Aristeas has for the temple and all that goes with it.

> For when we arrived at the places we saw the city lying in the middle of the whole of Judaea, on a mountain of considerable height. On the summit was built the Temple, having a prominent position. And there were three enclosed precincts over seventy cubits in size, the width and length being in proportion to the house as regards its structure. Everything was constructed on a grand scale and expense entirely surpassing everything else.[16]

If this did indeed relate to Zerubbabel's temple, and if there was some realism about it, then truly it was as the prophet Haggai affirmed:

> The latter splendour of this house shall be greater than the former, says the Lord of hosts … (Haggai 2.9a)

In the days of Solomon's temple, national leadership had been in the hands of a series of kings, Uzziah (767–740 BC, in the year of whose death Isaiah the prophet says he had his vision of the Lord: Isaiah 6), Jotham (740–732), Ahaz (732–716), and Hezekiah (716–687). Of Jotham we hear nothing, though probably passages early in the book of Isaiah that speak on the one hand of wealth and power, and on the other of comparative poverty and powerlessness (Isaiah 3.13–26; 5.11–13) come from the days of his reign. Concerning Ahaz's reign the incident that we hear the most about is the Syro-Ephraimite attack upon Jerusalem, an incident that for Isaiah manifests Ahaz's lack both of religious faith and also of elementary statecraft. It is Isaiah's hope that after those days both more-trusting in God and also better political counsels will prevail. As indeed they appear to have done in the reign of Ahaz's son and successor, Hezekiah. In that king's days the attack of Sennacherib, ruler of Assyria, on Jerusalem was withheld. Yet in the fulness of time the city did fall to the siege of Nebuchadnezzar who to make sure of his success set fire to the city, destroyed the temple, and deported many of its people to Babylon.

The historical setting of Isaiah 40 to 55 is that of Jerusalem in a poor and devastated condition. Yet the glowing promises of God are that neither is this city forgotten (49.14–18), and nor are those who are in exile (40.27–31). The exiles are about to be summoned to make the journey, something of a new exodus, to this city which is to become resplendent and beautiful (52.1–12).

The third part of the book of Isaiah, chapters 56 to 66, portrays a city that appears to be in a period of building and transition, in which there is no real peace. There are still the old problems of lack of justice and righteousness (58.1–9), and yet at the same time the possibilities under God of a good and beneficent future are more than alive (60.1–7; 61.8–11; 62.1–12).

Jerusalem in the book of Isaiah

There is no single picture of Jerusalem given in the book of Isaiah. Rather, there are several portrayals of the city, portrayals that may seem at first sight to be contradictory. In fact not only are they intended to portray different aspects of God's will and purpose for the city, but also frequently they come from different historical moments, though which particular historical moment gave rise to each of these is often not easy to determine. We may consider this portrayal of the city under at least four heads.

(1) First there is the **sinful city**, the city to which we are introduced at the very beginning of the book, the city in which there is no longer justice and righteousness, but the city whose life is directed and driven by bribes and gifts, where orphans and

widows are not cared for, and which has now become a place of
murders (Isaiah 1.21–23). This theme is there in 10.1–4, and also
in 24.10 where Jerusalem is described as 'the city of chaos' that
'is broken down'. In 33.14 the sinners in the city have become
afraid, the godless are seized with trembling, and are aware of the
(divine) consuming fire that now threatens them. In fact, such is
the sin of this city, so much is it under the judgement of God, that
in chapter 29 the Lord himself is portrayed as laying siege to his
city (here named and addressed as 'Altar hearth', the place of
burning) just as David had laid siege to it those centuries ago
(2 Samuel 5.6–10). So,

> Ah, Ariel, Ariel,
>   the city where David encamped!
> Add year to year;
>   let the festivals run their round.
> Yet I will distress Ariel,
>   and there shall be moaning and lamentation,
>   and Jerusalem shall be to me like an Ariel.
> And like David I will encamp against you;
>   I will besiege you with towers
>   and raise siege-works against you. (Isaiah 29.1–3)

Even later in the Isaiah book, in parts of chapters 56 to 66 this
theme of the sinful city of Jerusalem recurs, in particular in the
lament in 63.7—64.12. Here is an expression of the sinfulness of
the city, expressed as if in a prayer of confession in which the
Lord's mercy is implored (see especially Isaiah 64.8–12).

(2) Then second, a very different aspect to the city: it is to be
renewed. The city is to have a future, in fact a glorious future.
A central and dominating theme of chapters 40 to 55 is that the
Babylonian exile is to come to an end, for the exiles are forgiven
their sins (Isaiah 40.2), and may return home. Moreover the
ruined city is to be rebuilt:

> … who [the Lord, your Redeemer] says of Jerusalem,
>   'It shall be rebuilt',

and of the temple, 'Your foundation shall be laid.'
(Isaiah 44.28)

Jerusalem is to be prepared for this great new moment,

> Rouse yourself, rouse yourself!
> Stand up, O Jerusalem ... (Isaiah 51.17)

for a magnificent future awaits the city (52.1–2), here being
referred to as 'the holy city' (as also in 48.2). Thus Jerusalem's sen-
tinels are to be on the alert for the return of the Lord to Zion, while
in poetic and imaginative imagery the prophet hears the ruins of
the city breaking into singing in the excitement of the moment.

> Break forth together into singing,
>   you ruins of Jerusalem;
> for the Lord has comforted his people,
>   he has redeemed Jerusalem.
> The Lord has bared his holy arm
>   before the eyes of all the nations;
> and all the ends of the earth shall see
>   the salvation of our God. (Isaiah 52.9–10)

In the third part of the book, still the promise is there – perhaps
with the tacit acknowledgement that the rebuilding has not yet
been completed.

> Your ancient ruins shall be rebuilt;
>   you shall raise up the foundations of many
>   generations;
> you shall be called the repairer of the breach,
>   the restorer of streets to live in. (Isaiah 58.12)

And again in chapters 60 to 62, chapters in which the main content is about the rebuilding and future glorification of Jerusalem/
Zion we read:

> The descendants of those who oppressed you
>   shall come bending low to you,

and all who despised you
    shall bow down at your feet;
they shall call you the City of the Lord,
    the Zion of the Holy One of Israel.
    (Isaiah 60.14. See also 61.1–4; 62.1, 3–4, 10–12)

(3) Then third,[17] we should take note of the theme of Jerusalem being a city **at peace**, a city no longer caught up in the maelstrom of political and military events, no longer perpetually at the mercy of the forces and influences that tend to chaos and destruction. Thus, for example, early in the book we have the well-known passage about the internal peace of the messianic reign in 11.1–9 with its concluding assurance, 'They will not hurt or destroy/on all my holy mountain' (Isaiah 11.9b). It is here that we find the thrilling assurance:

The wolf shall live with the lamb,
    the leopard shall lie down with the kid,
the calf and the lion and the fatling together,
    and a little child shall lead them. (Isaiah 11.6)

Then some verses in Isaiah 33, a chapter I believe that was deliberately framed in the language and manner of worship, and which in a remarkable series of contrasts has verses about the grim reality of life on earth while others give expression to visions of peace. Here in 33.20–24 Jerusalem is portrayed as a place of quietness and peace, under the care of the God who is judge, lawgiver and king, the one who will save his people.[18]

Look on Zion, the city of our appointed festivals!
    Your eyes will see Jerusalem,
        a quiet habitation, an immovable tent,
whose stakes will never be pulled up,
    and none of whose ropes will be broken.
But there the Lord in majesty will be for us
    a place of broad rivers and streams,
where no galley with oars can go,

> nor stately ship can pass.
> For the Lord is our judge, the Lord is our ruler,
>> the Lord is our king; he will save us. (Isaiah 33.20–22)

Undoubtedly what we have here is an idealised picture of the city at peace, but it is nevertheless a vision that was intended to invite worshippers of Yahweh to share, so that they would have a positive and joyful anticipation of future peace and well being.

So we come to chapters 60 to 62, three chapters that in some senses stand at the heart of the message of Isaiah 56 to 66, making something of a core in the wider group of chapters, maybe even being the earliest material in chapters 56 to 66. [19] At any rate they spell out the wondrous effects of the ongoing promises and purposes of God, such things that become a possibility when there is faithfulness on the part of God's people, such as is spoken about in the immediately preceding chapter 59. Further, chapter 60 in particular speaks of the future glory of Zion, here addressed in the second person feminine as a woman who has been downtrodden and rejected, but whose situation in life and fortunes have suddenly been transformed (Isaiah 60.1–3). This will be the city of glory and wealth, and of peace, salvation and praise:

> Instead of bronze I will bring gold,
>> instead of iron I will bring silver;
> instead of wood, bronze,
>> instead of stones, iron.
> I will appoint Peace as your overseer
>> and Righteousness as your taskmaster.
> Violence shall be no more heard in your land,
>> devastation or destruction within your borders;
> you shall call your walls Salvation,
>> and your gates Praise. (Isaiah 60.17–18)

This coming day of peace, prosperity and glory is also spelled out in parts of the penultimate chapter of the whole book, chapter 65, which in remarkable language speaks of the peaceful future of the city, whose inhabitants will find delight in life. In this place

there will be found again the perfect covenant relationship
between God and his people. Here is the original paradise, now
restored and in which the baleful serpent is put firmly in its place.

> But be glad and rejoice for ever
> > in what I am creating;
> for I am about to create Jerusalem as a joy,
> > and its people as a delight.
> I will rejoice in Jerusalem,
> > and delight in my people;
> no more shall the sound of weeping be heard in it,
> > or the cry of distress....
> They shall build houses and inhabit them;
> > they shall plant vineyards and eat their fruit....
> Before they call I will answer,
> > while they are yet speaking I will hear.
> The wolf and the lamb shall feed together,
> > the lion shall eat straw like the ox;
> > but the serpent – its food shall be dust!
> They shall not hurt or destroy
> > on all my holy mountain,
> > > > says the Lord.
> (Isaiah 65.18–19, 21, 24–25)

(4) So in the fourth place to one other aspect of the city of
Jerusalem in the book of Isaiah, namely the city in which there is
Temple and Torah, the sanctuary and the divine instruction.
This is the city that is the religious centre. The sanctuary of this
city, Solomon's temple, would appear to be the setting of the
account of Isaiah's call to be a prophet (Isaiah 6.1–13), while temple (just which temple must remain a moot point, the dating of this
passage being a debated matter), city and mountain are envisaged
in Isaiah 2.2–4 as the focal point from which divine instruction
concerning life and religion go out into the wide world.

> In days to come
> > the mountain of the Lord's house

shall be established as the highest of the mountains,
and shall be raised above the hills;
all the nations shall stream to it.
Many peoples shall come and say,
'Come, let us go up to the mountain of the Lord,
to the house of the God of Jacob;
that he may teach us his ways
and that we may walk in his paths.'
For out of Zion shall go forth instruction,
and the word of the Lord from Jerusalem.
(Isaiah 2.2–3)

The prophet of chapters 40 to 55 does not speak of the restoration of temple and cult in Jerusalem, and we have to conclude from his silence that he was not greatly concerned about these things. Yet for this prophet there is no doubt that with the stirring events the Lord is setting in motion by bringing his people out of captivity, divine renown and glory are going out into a wide world (40.5; 49.26b). Different is the prophet, or the prophets, of chapters 56 to 66. In these chapters there is voiced a deep and heartfelt concern about the sanctuary that is both trampled down (63.18) and also burned (64.11). Here also is a vision of a renewed sanctuary (60.13), a sanctuary that in the new situation in which people find themselves will be both a house of prayer and a place for the offering of sacrifices for all.

And the foreigners who join themselves to the Lord,
to minister to him, to love the name of the Lord,
and to be his servants,
all who keep the sabbath, and do not profane it,
and hold fast my covenant –
these I will bring to my holy mountain,
and make them joyful in my house of prayer;
their burnt-offerings and their sacrifices
will be accepted on my altar;
for my house shall be called a house of prayer

for all peoples.
(Isaiah 56.6–7. See also 66.20–21, 23)

Jerusalem, Zion would seem to be the setting in which a prophet is called to announce to his people their rebellion and sin (58.1), and to call them to proper observance of the sabbath (58.13). Yet also within these chapters, it should be observed, any notion that a temple can 'house' God, 'contain' him, is firmly rejected.

> Thus says the Lord:
> Heaven is my throne
> and the earth is my footstool;
> what is the house that you would build for me,
> and what is my resting place?
> (Isaiah 66.1)

Reflections

It is striking that in the book of Isaiah there is such frequent reference to Jerusalm/Zion, and further that this occurs in all the three main parts of the book. The name Jerusalem occurs 49 times, Zion 46 times. In the case of Zion this frequency is approached only by the book of Psalms with 37 occurrences.[20] It is further striking that in Isaiah there are comparatively few references to other towns and cities in Judah, and that where there are they are generally of a circumstantial nature.[21]

Thus we have to say that the whole notion of Jerusalem as a special religious city is given serious emphasis in the book of Isaiah. Jerusalem does seem to have been for those responsible in their different ways for the Isaiah book the city of Yahweh, the 'holy city'.[22] At the same time, it has to be said that there is no thought in this book that Yahweh is bound to Jerusalem/Zion, or that he is the God of Jerusalem. Yet certainly in chapters 40 to 55 there is an address to Zion that stresses the intimate nature of the relationship between the Lord and this city, 'your God'. That is, in 52.7, for instance, we have 'your God': '… who says to Zion, "Your God reigns" '.[23]

While indeed Yahweh will fight for his city, in fact protect it (expressed in 31.5, and maybe also implied in 8.1–10), yet as we have seen this is the city that at times is under the severest judgement of the Lord. And no doubt the city of Jerusalem in its continuing history has been in many subsequent ages under the judgement of God. As no doubt many of the cities of humankind have in many an age been under the judgement of God, and all of these cities alike for their failures to provide shelter and life for all manner of people, especially the weaker ones of society, and also because of their being led in such hesitant and faulty ways. Further, it may perhaps appear that many a time Jerusalem and its people have been forgiven, and more, whether they knew it or not, have experienced the gift of renewal. And this not only for Jerusalem, but also for so many cities and towns throughout the world all down the ages.

For the rest of this piece I wish to reflect first upon the theme of Jerusalem as a place of worship and from which divine instruction goes out, and then second on this city as a place of peace, the city of peace. And though I may not specifically speak again of Jerusalem/Zion as the city under God's judgement, or as the city that becomes renewed by God, yet I would ask that as we continue, we do have those two themes somewhere at the back of our minds, to inform us and to infuse our thoughts of what now become my two major considerations – Jerusalem as religious centre, and Jerusalem as the city of peace.

First then, Jerusalem as the place of worship and from which divine instruction goes out, Jerusalem as religious centre. In the days of the eighth-century prophet Isaiah of Jerusalem, Solomon's temple stood in Jerusalem, no doubt something of an architectural and building wonder of the age, no doubt for its day a grandiose place in which grandiose worship took place. The interior of this temple appears to be the setting for Isaiah's vision of the holy God and of the divine retinue, all of which brought home to the prophet-to-be the unworthiness of himself and others (Isaiah 6). Externally, this temple and its successors crowned the city set on the hill, this city that could not be hidden. [24] And whoever was responsible for Isaiah 2.2–4 held the vision that there was something to do with the will of God, and of the divine instruction, that was to go out from here to surrounding areas, and even to other nations. According to Isaiah 2.2–3 'all nations will stream to it', that this may be the result:

> 'that he [the Lord] may teach us his ways
>> and that we may walk in his paths.'
> For out of Zion shall go forth instruction,
>> and the word of the Lord from Jerusalem.
> (Isaiah 2.3b)

Yet it has to be said that the eighth-century Isaiah of Jerusalem does not speak of the temple frequently, but whether this is because he is not deeply concerned about it, or because he is looking for a belief on the part of his people that is rooted elsewhere than in a building, or whether this is because he simply assumes that the temple is there and that it will continue to be there in Jerusalem, we do not know.

This temple of Solomon did indeed cease to exist in 587 BC, and for over half a century Judean people had to live without a temple. Was it this lack of temple that constituted one of the factors that made it difficult to worship the Lord in a strange land (Psalm 137.4)? In fact, had this psalmist been one of the temple musicians? [25] But then, the prophet of Isaiah 40 to 55 seems not to have any great or deep concern about a replacement temple for the old ruined Solomonic one. [26] This prophet although having a good deal to say about Jerusalem being rebuilt, does not express a like concern about a new temple. How can we account for this? Was it that he, and perhaps others, had learned to live, worship, and practise their faith without temple and sacrificial worship? Or was it because, by the time this prophet had begun to prophesy, the institution of the synagogue had come into being, so offering a new way of worship, one that was not centred on sacrifice? [27] Then again, what exile had done for Judean people was to take them into a wider world, and no doubt that had inevitably led them to experience both different ways of life and also different manners of worship from those known by them and their ancestors in times past.

While the prophet of Isaiah 40 to 55 may not appear to have any great concern about the building of a new temple in Jerusalem, he does seem to have envisaged the city as the centre from which a religious message went out to a wider world. The first two of the passages in these chapters about a servant concern the issues of mission to a wider world than that merely of people in Judah (Isaiah 42.1–4; 49.1–6). In spite of past failures in the living out of faith in the national setting, nevertheless here comes the call to go out into the international sphere. The 'coasts and islands' [28] are portrayed as waiting for, hungry for, this message concerning the Lord (42.4), and perhaps it is from around this time that the vision in Isaiah 2.2–5 is to be dated. To be noted in this oracle is the message for the wider world, and this will involve people coming to Jerusalem to be taught by the Lord, and thereby divine instruction will go out from there.

Yet in the fulness of time, a new temple was built in Jerusalem. Certainly those who were responsible for chapters 56 to 66 of the book were concerned about temple worship. But now there was to be, for these prophets, a temple that would be a 'house of prayer for all nations' (56.7). While the emphasis in this verse may be on this new temple as the place of prayer, yet at the same time the sacrificial worship aspect is not missing (56.7; 66.20). This temple of Zerubbabel was much rebuilt and extended by Herod. No doubt it was understood by at least some people as the meeting point of the divine and human realms, the particular point of intersection of God and his people. To this temple came the people with their psalms and prayers, with their sacrifices and offerings, while from this place it was believed went forth intimations of the divine will and the assurance of the Lord's forgiveness of sins.

Yet this rebuilt and expanded temple was to have only a short life, it being destroyed at the hands of the soldiers of the Roman Titus in AD 70. Henceforth the religion of Jewish people would be, and would remain, temple-less. Maybe there was a sense in

which the attitude of the prophet of Isaiah 40 to 55 came into its
own. Then also, Christians came to understand that for them the
meeting point between God and humanity was no longer in a
temple, but rather in and through Christ Jesus. Thus did they
understand the words of Jesus about destroying the temple and
rebuilding it in three days (Matthew 26.61; Mark 14.58), which in
John's Gospel has the explanatory statement that Jesus, 'was
speaking of the temple of his body' (John 2.21). So also did the
Gospel writers speak of the veil of the temple that stood before
the most holy and divinity-charged part of that holy place, as
being torn in two at the time of the crucifixion of Jesus (Matthew
27.51; Mark 15.38; Luke 23.45). John's Gospel does not speak of
this, but then he has the mother of Jesus (representing the old
community of God's people) being taken into the home ('house',
that is 'household') of the beloved disciple (representing the new
community of God's people: John 19.27). And nor should we
omit that thought expressed in Revelation 21.22 concerning the
absence of a temple building in the new Jerusalem. In this new
household of faith there is indeed to be a new dispensation, part
of which will have the new meeting point of God and his people
in God himself and the Lamb. Here, further, is the vision for a
peaceful future – the remembrance of which will serve to lead us
on to the other aspect of Jerusalem in the book of Isaiah that we
were to consider.

> I saw no temple in the city, for its temple is the Lord God
> the Almighty and the Lamb. And the city has no need of
> sun or moon to shine on it, for the glory of God is its light,
> and its lamp is the Lamb. The nations will walk by its
> light, and the kings of the earth will bring their glory into
> it. Its gates will never be shut by day – and there will be
> no night there. (Revelation 21.22–25)

So second, then, those visions, pictures in the book of Isaiah of
Jerusalem as a place of peace, the city where there is peace for all,
security and life for everyone, the place from which the message,
and also the reality, of peace will go out to other nations and

peoples (e.g. 2.4), and within whose walls will be those in positions of leadership who will make wise decisions that will assuredly lead to conditions of justice and righteousness (1.26–27).

> And I will restore your judges as at the first,
>> and your counsellors as at the beginning.
> Afterwards you shall be called the city of righteousness,
>> the faithful city. (Isaiah 1.26)

It is most likely that the swelling and exhuberant vision of 4.2–6 comes from post-exilic times, giving a picture of the city under divine protection, thus able to afford peace, security and protection to all who live within it.

> Then the Lord will create over the whole site of Mount Zion and over its places of assembly a cloud by day and smoke and the shining of a flaming fire by night. Indeed, over all the glory there will be a canopy. It will serve as a pavilion, a shade by day from the heat, and a refuge and a shelter from the storm and rain. (Isaiah 4.5–6)

In his great work, *City of God*, St Augustine speaks of the peace of the city, and of the mutual interaction there of the peace of individual families and that of the city. The peaceful city is where families find their peace, yet equally the peacefulness of those families contributes to the ongoing peace of the city. Thus,

> Now a man's house ought to be the beginning, or rather a small component part of the city, and every beginning is directed to some end of its own kind, and every component part contributes to the completeness of the whole of which it forms a part. The implication is quite apparent, that domestic peace contributes to the peace of the city – that is, the ordered harmony of those who live together in a house in the matter of giving and obeying orders, contributes to the ordered harmony concerning authority and obedience obtaining among the citizens. Consequently it is fitting that the father of a household

should take his rules from the law of the city, and govern
his household in such a way that it fits in with the peace
of the city.[29]

And in times nearer our own, and in our own culture, we may
recall how some of the Victorians held the vision of the city as
being the place of civilisation and peace. In Birmingham the
attempt was made by some to fashion the city along lines that
approximated to a divine society. Here there ministered the Revd
George Dawson who in 1844 became minister at the Mount Zion
Chapel, in 1874 taking up the same post at the Church of the
Saviour on Edward Street. Dawson, 'imagined the modern city
as an organic whole whose purpose was to secure an ideal of
the good life for all its citizens.'[30] A contemporary described
Dawson's vision of the city thus:

> For a city, as he conceived it, was a society, established by
> the divine will, as the family, the State, and the Church
> are established, for common life and common purpose
> and common action.[31]

It was religious leaders such as Dawson, along with the likes of
R. W. Dale the minister of Carrs Lane Chapel, and H. Crosskey
the Unitarian minister of the Church of the Messiah, who
inspired Joseph Chamberlain, a member of Crosskey's congregation, to carry through their vision into the reality of the city's life.
'The preacher infused the minds of the people with municipal
reform, while Chamberlain, "the cool, calm man of business, the
long-headed, persevering, patient, yet acute politician", had the
guile to see it through.'[32]

And while we are in this vein we may perhaps go back a century and spare a thought for William Blake (1757–1827) and his
visions of the life of people in their societies. In his lifetime Blake
was regarded by many as a somewhat insane, though gifted, individual. Yet he strove to take a stand for spiritual matters in the
face of what he saw as the narrow vision and growing material-
ism of his age. His particular *bêtes noires* were Joshua Reynolds,

John Locke and Isaac Newton, for he was concerned to give a
prophetic warning of the perils of a world that was understood
merely in mechanistic terms with men and women being no more
than cogs in an industrial revolution. The Christian poet W. H.
Auden would come to appreciate Blake, share some of his *bêtes
noires*, and come to understand that here was a man who felt the
presence of God and spiritual realities all around him. In his
'New Year Letter' of 1940 Auden wrote of,

> Self-educated William Blake
> Who threw his spectre in the lake,
> Broke off relations in a curse
> With the Newtonian Universe,
> But even as a child would pet
> The tigers Voltaire never met,
> Took walks with them through Lambeth, and
> Spoke to Isaiah in the Strand,
> And heard inside each mortal thing
> Its holy emanation sing ...[33]

And perhaps in that sort of spirit we may hear again the well-
known words of Blake about the Jerusalem that he desired to see
in the increasingly industrialised Britain of his day. Is there perhaps something here that is owing to one of the conversations in
the Strand between William Blake and Isaiah of Jerusalem?

> And did those feet in ancient time
> Walk upon Englands mountains green:
> And was the holy Lamb of God,
> On Englands pleasant pastures seen!
>
> And did the Countenance Divine,
> Shine forth upon our clouded hills?
> And was Jerusalem builded here,
> Among those dark Satanic Mills? [34]

And finally, what of Jerusalem today? In particular what of
Jerusalem and the Isaianic visions of it being a religious centre

and a city of peace? As far as the first is concerned, it is certainly the holy city not any longer just for the Jewish faith, but now also for both Christians and Muslims. All three of these monotheistic faiths look to Jerusalem as something of a mother city, a place to which many of their devotees go on pilgrimage, looking to it as a centre of religious life, a source of inspiration. Yet tragically it is no city of peace. As Karen Armstrong, with whom I began, says,

> Yet from the first, Zion was never merely a physical entity. It was also an ideal. From the Jebusite period, Zion was revered as a city of peace, an earthly paradise of harmony and integration. The Israelite psalmists and prophets also developed this vision. Yet Zionist Jerusalem today falls sadly short of the ideal. Ever since the Crusades, which permanently damaged relations between the three religions of Abraham, Jerusalem has been a nervous, defensive city. It has also, increasingly, been a contentious place. Not only have Jews, Christians, and Muslims fought and competed with one another there, but violent sectarian strife has divided the three main communities internally into bitter warring factions.[35]

And a little further she says,

> Today Israelis and Arabs have to decide whether they want peace or victory in Jerusalem. The prophet Isaiah had a very different millennial vision for the holy city. He looked forward to a time when the wolf and the lamb, the panther and the kid – creatures who had previously existed in a state of deadly hostility with one another – would lie down together on God's Holy Mountain. If, after decades of bloody strife, the Israelis and Palestinians could achieve a similar coexistence in Jerusalem, Zion would indeed become a light to all nations and a beacon of hope.[36]

POSTLUDE: A SERMON

Yesterday, today and tomorrow

Isaiah 61.1–3; Luke 4.16–30

For all of us there is the matter of yesterday, today and tomorrow in our lives. We do our best to heed the instruction of our Lord to live just for today, but for most of us there is yesterday with all its baggage of experiences and relationships that have shaped us, making us to at least some extent the people we are today. And although we are told not to worry about tomorrow we are conscious that soon it will be here, and that brings a sense either of anticipation, or excitement, or concern. Yesterday, today and tomorrow, for good or ill, are always around us.

But the particular yesterday, today and tomorrow that I am thinking about are these. For our scripture readings today we read first a passage from the book of Isaiah that was from a yesterday, and second one from St Luke's Gospel where we are told that after he had read from the book of the prophet Isaiah Jesus' very first words were, 'Today this scripture has been fulfilled in your hearing.' And tomorrow? Well, if this present sermon is any good, and if it is to be of any help, then it must make us think about tomorrow and consider how we are going to live out our faith – tomorrow.

So first, Yesterday. And this yesterday must have been at least two thousand five hundred years ago – some would say that it was written even longer ago than that. Anyway, it was a good while ago. But in that time God called a prophet to announce to his people good news, good news for the oppressed, something good for those who were broken hearted, a liberating message for those who felt that they were imprisoned, kept captive, in their present lives.

And it does look as if those people needed a message like that. It does seem that the last eleven chapters of the book of Isaiah come from the time after God's people had returned from exile in Babylon and elsewhere. Through the good and favourable Persian ruler's decree that subject peoples could go back to their homelands and worship their own gods, all looked set for a great new beginning for Jewish people. They could go back to Jerusalem! It was as if the war was over and, praise be, they could go home. But alas! It seems that Jerusalem was not quite what they had expected, but was ruinous, run down, broken down. It needed a new temple, and no doubt it needed a lot of other new things as well. Hardly a place fit for the heroes coming home from half a century of exile!

We can well understand that a prophet was called by the Lord to bring good news to such oppressed people, to bind up those whose hearts were breaking because of all the ruin that they saw around them, who felt captive in a rather unpromising situation.

And the prophet also said this: That in fact *this* moment was, under God, really rather a special and significant moment – it was the year of the Lord's favour. I think that what the prophet meant was that *that* time, *that* moment, *that* year, was God's special time, moment, year for those people in that situation – in the sense that in fact any time and all times, any moment and all moments, any year and all years, are special in our lives under God wherever we are – in the sense that *this* is the time, the moment, the year when we are called to live the life of faith in this setting here. *This*, for us, is the time of the Lord's favour.

How wonderful, I used to think at one time, to have been a minister in the days when the churches and the chapels were full. But I put away such childish thoughts as I came to realise that I was called to be a minister in *these* years, and that as far as my life is concerned, and all that I am called to be and to do as a follower of Christ, *this* is the year of the Lord's favour. Let us rejoice and be glad in this time!

That was yesterday, but already I have been talking about today. But then, what is now yesterday was once today, and that yesterday of the returned exiles to Jerusalem was for them a truly challenging today in their lives.

So here is another Today: That day when Jesus went to the synagogue in Nazareth, and when they invited him to read from the book of the prophet Isaiah and to say a word to the congregation. And what happened went something like this. Jesus read the words of the book of Isaiah that had been intended to be a message for people who lived about five centuries earlier, he read those words, and having rolled up the scroll and handed it back to the attendant, Jesus made his great announcement: 'Today this scripture has been fulfilled in your hearing.'

That is, Jesus was saying that with him, and through him, through God working in him, there would be new dimensions of life available for those who felt themselves to be held captive, new possibilities for those who felt oppressed and held down by the present circumstances of their lives. And Jesus was also saying that there in that time, that moment, there was once again that time of specialness and significance. It was God's special time, it was the time of the Lord's favour, the year of the Lord's favour. Now of course we know, and we all accept, that what happened in the life of Jesus on earth was very special, and that in him God was at work in *the* most special ways.

And yet, as Jesus took that passage from Isaiah – already five hundred, or even more, years old – the wording began to change. In the first place, because it was the sabbath-day worship in the synagogue Jesus read from the Hebrew scroll of Isaiah, in Hebrew. But when Luke wrote up this story in his Gospel – without which we would not know about this incident! – Luke wrote in Greek, and the verses from Isaiah that Luke quoted were in the Greek translation of the Hebrew Scriptures. And not only was that Greek translation of the Hebrew a bit different here and there from the Hebrew, but also – and this in the second place – Luke added a few words of his own into the whole thing. And all this because the world for which Luke wrote was Greek speaking, not Hebrew speaking. Or at least, those people that Luke wanted to reach with his Gospel had Greek as their common language, not Hebrew, and so Luke needed to update the message for his own age.

And that is just what Jesus had done. Jesus had taken the five hundred year old – or more – words from the book of the prophet Isaiah and had said to the congregation, 'Today this scripture has been fulfilled in your hearing.' That is, Jesus was taking the old message and applying it for his 'today' – and Luke then added his own ten pen'oth to make it relevant for *his* 'today'.

And with that in mind, please consider Tomorrow – I mean *our* Tomorrow. I mean the tomorrow where *we* shall be, a tomorrow where we are unlikely to meet any people who speak in Hebrew, or who speak Greek. If we meet church or chapel people then we shall be with people who know something about the Bible, but very likely most of the people we shall meet will not know much at all that is in the Bible.

Naturally, the Bible is so important to us. It is one of the great links between us and the source of the faith of the Church, a faith that we now share. But if we are going to say something in our communities today about the things of our faith, then we have got to try to find new words with which to express it all. It's no good us just quoting the Bible out there!

It thrills and encourages me when I hear stories of those who are reaching out to people who in the past have not had contact with the Church. I rejoice that there are 'alternative churches' where the church thing happens all informally in a café, or a sitting room, or on skateboards, or in some other way or setting. Here are our people who in our today are trying to take the things that have been believed, and practised, and lived by – those things of the faith that have both challenged and also encouraged generations of people – here are people who in their own today are trying to communicate, to pass on, something of the wonder of these things for another generation. Those who seek to do such things need and deserve our prayers, our encouragement, and our warmest support.

And what shall *we* do tomorrow? Perhaps it is fairly clear for us in our lives how we shall live out the ancient faith of the

Church in our world of the twenty-first century. But who knows what may happen, and who we may meet? Who knows, we may come into contact with someone, or a family, with no contact with the Church. We shall be aware of the language problem between us, and perhaps we shall feel that all that we can do is to try to make our own little acts of care, concern and love, a bit like the Master did all those centuries ago. Or, just possibly, we might have the opportunity to, say, make a stand for justice in our world – especially for those who have so little, and for those who seem to count for so little in the great affairs of the world. And then, with our stand for justice in the world – fair shares for all – we really would be taking words from the book of the prophet Isaiah of many *yesterdays* ago, words that were perhaps recorded by someone or some people for their own *today*, and we would be applying them in our lives and in our world *tomorrow*.

And then, who knows, some little seed (if I may use the language of the Bible here in this setting), some little seed of the ancient faith, belief and practice that comes to us from many *yesterdays* ago, and which we are a part of *today*, may *tomorrow* be shared again and may by God's grace and in his purposes yield a harvest.

> Glory be to the Father,
> and to the Son,
> and to the Holy Spirit.
> As it was in the beginning,
> is now and ever shall be,
> world without end. Amen.

NOTES

Preface

1 Francis Watson ed., *The Open Text: New Directions for Biblical Studies?*, London, SCM Press, 1993, p. 3. Luther's words cited in my text above may be found in *Luther's Works, Vol. 10, First Lectures on the Psalms I (Psalms 1-75)*, ed. H. C. Oswald, Saint Louis, Concordia Publishing House, 1974, p. 7.

Prelude

1 In this work I retain the traditional Christian Church terminology, Old Testament, New Testament, BC, AD. Though alternative forms such as Hebrew Bible, BCE and so on, have their own particularly appropriate usage, here I am writing for the Christian community and about its use of its earliest Scriptures, namely the Jewish Hebrew Bible, which it inherited and which became for the Christian Church the first part of its Scriptures, that is the Old Testament, the second part being the New Testament. Thus the traditional Christian Church nomenclature seems appropriate in this present context.

2 Karl Jaspers spoke of this as an 'axial age' (in English translation, K. Jaspers, *The Origin and Goal of History*, London, Routledge & Kegan Paul, 1953), and apropos the Old Testament prophets J. Blenkinsopp says, 'As generally understood, the concept states that there occurred in the course of the first millennium B.C.E. in various parts of the world, including Greece and Israel, a breakthrough to a coherent vision of a transcendental reality and a construction of the world in keeping with it. Essential to the form it took in Israel was the conviction of a personal, ethical deity, whose demands, arising out of his very nature, led to a voluntary, contractual relationship between deity and people, the creation of an autonomous sphere of law, and an emphasis on human accountability.' (J. Blenkinsopp, *Sage, Priest, Prophet: Religious and Intellectual Leadership in Ancient Israel*, Louisville, Kentucky, Westminster John Knox Press, 1995, pp. 144-45).

3 It is possible to see the nature of such a scroll, indeed a facsimile of a scroll of the book of Isaiah which was found in one of the caves of the Qumran community on the shore of the Dead Sea, in the 'Shrine of the Book' at the Israel Museum in Jerusalem. See below, p. 104.

4 These are W. F. Albright's dates. See Blenkinsopp, *Isaiah 1–39*, p. 105. See also Stacey, *Isaiah 1–39*, p. xx, for a note about the different chronologies of scholars for these reigns.

5 Others would use the terms 'editors' and 'redactors' in different senses. See, for example T. Collins, *The Mantle of Elijah: The Redaction Criticism of the Prophetical Books* (The Biblical Seminar), Sheffield, JSOT Press, 1993, p. 32. However, in this present work I use them indiscriminately.

6 For the names 'Israel', 'Judah', and others, in the book of Isaiah see my comments on Isaiah 1.3: see below pp. 10-11.

7 For further details see below, p. 104.

Part One

1 This was originally propounded by G. Fohrer in an article, 'Jesaja 1 als Zusammenfassung der Verkündigung Jesajas', *ZAW* 74 (1962), pp. 251-268.

2 See Isaiah 41.1-5, 21-29; 43.8-13; 44.6-8, 21-22; 45.20-25. See, Stacey, *Isaiah 1–39*, p. 2; Thompson, *Isaiah 40–66*, p. xxvi.

3 See Isaiah chapter 37, and about this see below pp. 57-62.

4 As we are well aware the book of Isaiah does not have the monopoly of giving us exaggerated statements in order to make a point. What about Mark 10.25?

5 It does have to be said that there is no absolutely clear way to determine what we have in any given passage in the book of Isaiah records the actual words of the prophet of that name. We have to face up to the fact that it appears to have been over a long period of time that the processes took place that were eventually to result in the book of Isaiah, and that during that long time changes could well have taken place in the accounts that were handed down. Further, in the light of new and different situations, older stories may well have come to be written up with rather different emphases. Decisions as to just what does and what does not come from Isaiah must inevitably be subjective, and thus scholars come up with different answers. However, we should not think that

because we deem certain words to be non-Isaianic that thereby they are less important than the 'authentic' ones. Rather, as well as being interested in what may be those 'authentic' words we are also interested in the completed book and in the whole of its contents. Moreover, it is the whole of the book that has been accepted as canonical scripture and that we now read in our Bibles.

6 For details see Stacey, *Isaiah 1–39*, pp. 13-15.

7 See note 5 above.

8 At a technical level this is referred to as diachronic and synchronic readings of a written document. A diachronic (from the Greek for 'through time') reading is where we take account of the time, or the times, from which a piece of writing comes. The synchronic (from the Greek for 'same time') approach is to look at the whole of a piece of writing as it stands at one particular point in its history, usually in its final form. With material from the Bible in the form in which we read it, it has become a part of the canon of Scripture.

9 See, for example, Clements, *Isaiah 1–39*, p. 53; Stacey, *Isaiah 1–39*, p. 29.

10 See, for example, Stacey, *Isaiah 1–39*, p. 34: 'It may be said that this theology lacks the theme of redeeming love. Indeed it does, but the book of Isaiah and the prophetic corpus need to be read as a whole.'

11 Blenkinsopp, *Isaiah 1–39*, p. 222.

12 Stacey, *Isaiah 1–39*, p. 46.

13 B. S. Childs, *Isaiah* (Old Testament Library), Louisville, Kentucky, Westminster John Knox Press, 2001, pp. 56-57.

14 M. E. W. Thompson, *Situation and Theology: Old Testament Interpretations of the Syro-Ephraimite War*, Sheffield, Almond Press, 1982, p. 50.

15 The Syro-Ephraimite war is also spoken about in 2 Kings 16 and 2 Chronicles 28, and maybe also in Hosea 5.8—7.16. See Thompson, *Situation and Theology* cited in the previous note.

16 On this see my *Situation and Theology*, pp. 58-59, cited above.

17 See Stacey, *Isaiah 1–39*, pp. 55-57; M. E. W. Thompson, 'Isaiah's Sign of Immanuel', *ExpTim* 95 (1983-4), pp. 67-71.

18 Stacey, *Isaiah 1–39*, p. 70.

19 See M. E. W. Thompson, 'Isaiah's Ideal King', *JSOT* 24 (1982), pp. 79-88.

20 See pp. 113-126 below.

21 For some details of this see, Stacey, *Isaiah 1–39*, p. 84; Thompson, *Situation and Theology*, p. 18.

22 For these psalm types, individual and communal thanksgivings, and others, see e.g. J. Day, *Psalms* (Old Testament Guides), Sheffield, JSOT Press, 1990; A. Curtis, *Psalms* (Epworth Commentary), Peterborough, Epworth Press, 2004, pp. xxviii-xxxi.

23 So Blenkinsopp, *Isaiah 1–39*, p. 270.

24 The case of the prophet Jonah in the book of Jonah is different. He is portrayed as having been called by the Lord to go and preach in Nineveh, the capital city of Assyria. But we do not read anywhere else in the Old Testament of this mission of Jonah, and it seems most likely that we are intended to understand this book as voicing a criticism of the people of Israel who, while believing that the Lord God of Israel is the God of the whole earth, have at the same time been singularly backward is engaging in a mission to the wider world. See M. E. W. Thompson, 'The Mission of Jonah', *ExpTim* 105 (1993-94), pp. 233-36. However, later in the book of Isaiah we shall need to give attention to what is said about the call of a servant to an international mission. See below on Isaiah 42.1-4 and 49.1-6.

25 Stacey, *Isaiah 1–39*, p. 98.

26 See Seitz, *Isaiah 1–39*, p. 169.

27 See L. L. Grabbe, *Judaism from Cyrus to Hadrian*, London, SCM Press, 1994, pp. 266-67.

28 See Grabbe in the work cited in the preceding note, pp. 54-55, 138-39.

29 For a treatment of apocalyptic material as found in the Bible, C. Rowland, *The Open Heaven: A Study of Apocalyptic in Judaism and Early Christianity*, London, SPCK, 1982, may be recommended.

30 Seitz, *Isaiah 1–39*, p. 172.

31 These quotations both come from Augustine, *City of God*, in the Bettenson translation in the Penguin Classics series, London, 1972, 1984, Book XIV, 13 (p. 573) and Book XIV, 28 (p. 593) respectively.

32 C. K. Barrett says about this expression, 'Creation ... is in bondage to corrupt powers, and this bondage is inevitably corrupting.' *A Commentary on the Epistle to the Romans*, London, A. & C. Black, Second Edition, 1991, p. 156.

33 O. Plöger, *Theocracy and Eschatology*, Oxford, Blackwell, 1968, p. 66.

34 The word 'predominates' is important here. As we have seen, there are parts of chapters 2 to 12 that come from times later than the eighth century BC, for example 2.2-4; 4.2-6. Yet the historical incident that predominates in these chapters, and that is reflected in various parts of this material, is the Syro-Ephraimite war.

35 See once again, Thompson, *Situation and Theology*, pp. 79-103.

36 On these psalms see, for example, A. Curtis, *Psalms* (Epworth Commentary), Peterborough, Epworth Press, 2004, pp. 101-106.

37 Blenkinsopp, *Isaiah 1–39*, p. 435, for example says, 'Ch. 33 presents the reader with a disjointed and uneven sequence of mostly brief passages.'

38 See M. E. W. Thompson, 'Vision, Reality and Worship: Isaiah 33', *ExpTim* 113 (2001-2002), pp. 327-333, where I argue for this sort of understanding of this chapter.

39 See e.g. Blenkinsopp, *Isaiah 1–39*, p. 450; Clements, *Isaiah 1–39*, p. 271; P. D. Miscall, *Isaiah 34-35: A Nightmare/A Dream*, Sheffield, JSOTSup 281, 1999.

40 Though Blenkinsopp (see preceding note) thinks the echoes are of chapters 56-66.

41 See Isaiah 5.6, 17; 7.23-25; 13.20-22; 14.22-23; 17.2; 27.10; 32.14. For a specialised treatment of this topic see K. Nielsen, *There is Hope for a Tree: The Tree as Metaphor in Isaiah*, Sheffield, JSOTSup 65, 1989.

42 See Thompson, *Isaiah 40–66*, pp. 155-157.

43 Other references to writing, or to a written document, in the book of Isaiah are 29.11, 12; 34.4; 37.14; 39.1; 50.1.

44 Thus, observes Wildberger, 'It would be interesting to know to which time this redactor belongs, which means, how old is this understanding that what is transmitted in the Bible is to be seen as Holy Scripture (cf. John 5.39)?' H. Wildberger, *Isaiah 28–39* (Continental Commentary), tr. T. H. Trapp, Minneapolis, Fortress Press, 2002, p. 338.

45 For a brief discussion of the imagery and language found in Isaiah 40-55, see Thompson, *Isaiah 40-66*, pp. xxvii-xxviii.

46 It is to be observed that in regard to Isaiah 36-39 Stacey and I take rather different viewpoints. Stacey says concerning 36.1-39.8, 'The presence of this section, inserted after chs 34-35, obscures the link which chapters 34-35 make between the first part of the book of Isaiah and the second.' See Stacey, *Isaiah 1–39*, p. 214. The point

that I and others seek to make is that chapters 36-39 have in fact been fashioned so as to provide a link between the first part of the book of Isaiah and the second. Further, I am also concerned with the presence of this material in the book of Isaiah for the reason that all that we have unearthed so far about the book suggests that it has very purposefully been edited, redacted into the final form that we now know. That is, there must surely be good reason why these chapters that, as we shall shortly see, having been taken from sources connected with those who were responsible for the books of Kings, have been adapted and incorporated into the book of Isaiah. This is to say that as well as being in the books of Kings they are also in the book of Isaiah and presumably thereby intended to be taken seriously in that setting.

47   This is not to say that what we have in Kings was the 'original'. Maybe there was an even earlier 'original', but we do not know one way or the other.

48   Those who wish to go into detail about this, and who have some facility with Hebrew, will find these Kings and Isaiah passages set out in Hebrew in parallel columns with helpful indications of the additions, subtractions and other changes, in H. Wildberger, *Isaiah 28–39* (Continental Commentary), tr. T. H. Trapp, Minneapolis, Fortress Press, 2002, pp. 481-493.

49   For these prayers of lament see M. E. W. Thompson, *I Have Heard Your Prayer: The Old Testament and Prayer*, Peterborough, Epworth Press, 1996, pp. 41-56, 210-12; also my 'Praying with the Old Testament: "Have Mercy ... O God" ', *Epworth Review* 31 (2004), pp. 35-43, esp. pp. 39-42.

50   However a minority of scholars argue for the addressees being people in Jerusalem rather than in Babylon. See, for example, M. D. Goulder, 'Deutero-Isaiah of Jerusalem', *JSOT* 28 (2004), pp. 351-362.

51   Thompson, *Isaiah 40-66*. See esp. p. xix.

52   There are those who understand the passages in Isaiah 40 to 55 about the servant (42.1-4; 49.1-6; 50.4-9; 52.13-53.12) as being autobiographical, having reference to the prophet himself. As we shall come to see below this is not the approach in this work, nor in Thompson, *Isaiah 40–66*, pp. xxiii-xxiv.

53   L. Alonso Schökel 'Isaiah', pp. 165-183, in *The Literary Guide to the Bible*, ed. R. Alter and F. Kermode, London, Collins, 1987, p. 174.

For examples of these 'four-part parallelisms' see 41.18; 52.11 etc. Blenkinsopp also uses the word 'rhetorical' of these chapters, having a sub-section within the Introduction with the title, 'Rhetorical Resources': see Blenkinsopp, *Isaiah 40–55*, pp. 61-65. See also what R. Alter has to say about 'Deutero-Isaiah, the great master of the poetry of redemption' (p. 157) in his *The Art of Biblical Poetry*, Edinburgh, T & T Clark, 1990, pp. 157-162.

54 For further details see Thompson, *Isaiah 40–66*, pp. xxvi-xxviii.

55 For this 'exodus' language and the thinking behind it, see Thompson, *Isaiah 40–66*, pp. 19-22.

56 The most thoroughgoing treatment of this question in the twentieth century was that of C. R. North, *The Suffering Servant in Deutero-Isaiah: An Historical and Critical Study*, Oxford, Oxford University Press, 1948, 1956.

57 R. N. Whybray, *Isaiah 40–66*; R. N. Whybray, *Thanksgiving for a Liberated Prophet: An Interpretation of Isaiah Chapter 53*, JSOTSup 4, 1978.

58 More recently, Blenkinsopp has argued that the servant is the prophet himself, but that the fourth passage was completed by a disciple. Blenkinsopp, *Isaiah 40–55*, pp. 76-81.

59 And also in Thompson, *Isaiah 40–66*.

60 Until Duhm it was common to find theories that had different servants in the four passages. See North, *Suffering Servant*, p. 46.

61 What is presented in these passages about the servant in Isaiah 40 to 55 is indeed radical when observed in the context of Israelite history as that is portrayed in the Old Testament. The preamble, the introductory words, to the Ten Commandments in Exodus 20.2 have the Lord affirming, 'I am the Lord your God who brought you out of the land of Egypt, from the house of bondage (literally, 'slavery, servanthood')' Now here with Second Isaiah is the reuse for the new situation of the old language of exodus, including the stark warning that the future will involve 'slavery, servanthood' (the same word as is used in Exodus 20.2, and frequently elsewhere in the book of Exodus)!

62 In Isaiah 41.22; 42.9; 43.9, 18; 46.9; 48.3 we have the expression 'former things … latter things' (or similar words). It would appear that these 'things' are not the same 'things' in all the references. In at least some of these occurrences the 'former things' are the events of the exodus from Egypt while the 'latter things' are

forthcoming new exodus events from Babylon to Jerusalem. See further, Thompson, *Isaiah 40–66*, pp. 23-24.

63 It has to be said that the prophet of Isaiah 40 to 55 does not display any great interest in the temple and its rebuilding. However that concern will come to the fore in chapters 56 to 66. See Isaiah 63.18; 64.11.

64 The apparent equation in verse 9 of the 'wicked' and the 'rich' has for long ages caused difficulties. See Thompson, *Isaiah 40–66*, p. 106.

65 It will be noted that here in Isaiah 55.13 we have yet another occurrence of the 'brier, thorn' imagery. But now all is transformed, and thorns and briers have been replaced by the cypress and the myrtle.

66 This is also the working hypothesis in my *Isaiah 40–66*; see p. xxix.

67 See R. E. Clements, *Old Testament Prophecy: From Oracles to Canon*, Louisville, Kentucky, Westminster John Knox Press, 1996, p. 201.

68 On this name of God, and this title, see Blenkinsopp, *Isaiah 56–66*, pp. 90-91; Thompson, *Isaiah 40–66*, pp. 168, 161, 164.

69 For example, J. Blenkinsopp, 'The "Servants of the Lord" in Third Isaiah', pp. 392-412 in R. P. Gordon, ed., *'The Place Is Too Small for Us': The Israelite Prophets in Recent Scholarship*, Winona Lake, Indiana, Eisenbrauns, 1995; W. A. M. Beuken, 'The Main Theme of Trito-Isaiah: The "Servants of YHWH"', *JSOT* 47 (1990), pp. 67-87.

70 Another example of such a change in meaning of a word between Isaiah 40 to 55 and 56 to 66 occurs with 'way'. In 40.3 'way' refers to the 'road, highway' through the desert for the purposes of God and the progress of his people for their pilgrimage to Jerusalem, whereas in 57.14-21 it is rather the 'way of life' in which God's people are called to go, that is intended to be their 'way of faith', their destined path in life. See Thompson, *Isaiah 40–66*, pp. 131-134 for further details.

71 Blenkinsopp, *Isaiah 56–66*, p. 83.

72 For Solomon's prayer of dedication of the temple, and its significance, see my, *I Have Heard Your Prayer: The Old Testament and Prayer*, Peterborough, Epworth Press, pp. 179-196.

73 B. S. Childs, *Isaiah* (Old Testament Library), Louisville, Kentucky, Westminster John Knox Press, 2001, p. 459.

74 For the thesis that Isaiah 1 sets out themes found throughout the book of Isaiah and that it is mirrored by chapter 66, see for

example, Clements, *Isaiah 1–39*, p. 28; M. A. Sweeney, *Isaiah 1–4 and the Post-exilic Understanding of the Isaianic Tradition*, Berlin, de Gruyter, 1988; A. J. Tomasino, 'Isaiah 1.1-2.4 and 63-66 and the Composition of the Isaianic Corpus', *JSOT* 57 (1993), pp. 81-98.

75 Blenkinsopp, *Isaiah 56–66*, pp. 299-301.

76 For details and references see Thompson, *Isaiah 40–66*, pp. 174-175.

77 Again, for fuller details see Thompson, *Isaiah 40–66*, pp. 175-176.

78 Blenkinsopp, *Isaiah 56–66*, p. 316, says, 'We may also be hearing an echo of the "name better than sons and daughters" promised to the sexually mutilated in 56:5.'

79 The book of Isaiah opened with 'new moon and sabbath' (1.13), but there used in a condemnatory sense, while 'all flesh' reminds of earlier usages of the expression in 40.5, 6; 49.26; 66.16.

80 B. S. Childs, *Isaiah* (Old Testament Library), Louisville, Kentucky, Westminster John Knox Press, p. 547.

81 Translation by John Mason Neale (1818–66) and others of eighteenth-century Latin hymn, *Veni veni Emmanuel*. In the first verse of this hymn we have echoes from the book of Isaiah, in particular Isaiah 7.14; 35.10; 59.20; 61.1.

Intermezzo

1 R. E. Clements says of the book of Isaiah, 'It is, I firmly believe, one of the most complex literary structures of the entire Old Testament.' *Old Testament Prophecy: From Oracles to Canon*, Louisville, Kentucky, Westminster John Knox Press, 1996, p. 81. The essay from which that quotation comes was first published as 'Beyond Tradition-History: Deutero-Isaianic Development of First Isaiah's Themes', *JSOT* 31 (1985), pp. 95-113.

2 C. R. Seitz, *Reading and Preaching the Book of Isaiah*, ed. C. R. Seitz, Philadelphia, Fortress Press, 1988, p. 108. For a recent study of the redaction of the prophetical books, see T. Collins, *The Mantle of Elijah: The Redaction Criticism of the Prophetical Books* (The Biblical Seminar), Sheffield, JSOT Press, 1993, especially pp. 37-58, 'A Book Called Isaiah'.

3 I have deliberately not used the word 'original' here, because we do not know just what written documents lay behind the present parts of the book, much less what there might have been *originally*.

4 A recent overview of some proposals as to the process by which the book of Isaiah assumed its present form is to be found in the

essay of M. E. Tate, 'The Book of Isaiah in recent Study', pp. 22-56 in *Forming Prophetic Literature: Essays on Isaiah and the Twelve in Honor of John D.W. Watts*, ed. J. W. Watts and P. R. House, JSOTSup 235, Sheffield 1996.

5 R. E. Clements is not convinced about the value of this 'disciple', 'school' nomenclature for the reason that, as he says, 'Their existence over a period of at least two centuries is postulated without any clear identification of where, or how, such a group maintained itself.' See his *Old Testament Prophecy: From Oracles to Canon*, Louisville, Kentucky, Westminster John Knox Press, 1996, p. 94. This quotation occurred originally in his article 'The Unity of the Book of Isaiah', *Int* 36 (1982), pp. 117-129. Yet, we may ask, how else are we to describe the phenomenon that resulted in the book of Isaiah?

6 *The Wisdom of Ben Sirach* (Anchor Bible), P. W. Skehan and A. A. Di Lella, New York, Doubleday, 1987, pp. 8-16; I. H. Jones, *The Apocrypha* (Epworth Commentary), Peterborough, Epworth Press, 2003, p. 97.

7 For introduction to the Qumran Scrolls see G. Vermes, *An Introduction to the Complete Dead Sea Scrolls*, London, SCM Press, 1999, and for the texts the same author's *The Complete Dead Sea Scrolls in English*, Sheffield, JSOT Press, 1987. Also see *The Dead Sea Scrolls in Their Historical Context*, ed. T. H. Lim with L. W. Hurtado, A. G. Auld, and A. Jack, Edinburgh, T & T Clark, 2000; J. Blenkinsopp, *Isaiah 1-39*, pp. 76-78, 'The Text of Isaiah and the Ancient Versions'.

8 William Williams (1717–91), tr. H. A. Hodge (1905–76); 417 in *Hymns and Psalms*, 1983.

Part Two

1 See pp. 57-62 above for details.

2 See M. E. W. Thompson, 'Vision, Reality and Worship: Isaiah 33', *ExpTim* 113 (2001-2002), pp. 327-333. See above, pp. 52-54.

3 For details of these 'servant' passages see above pp. 70-81.

4 See H. G. M. Williamson, *Variations on a Theme: King, Messiah and Servant in the Book of Isaiah* (Didsbury Lectures), Carlisle, Paternoster Press, 1998.

5 See S. H. Evans in G. S. Wakefield, ed., *A Dictionary of Christian Spirituality*, London, SCM Press, 1983, p. 13.

6 J. S. Pobee, in the same work, p. 5, though I have taken the liberty of changing his 'man' to 'people'.

7 G. S. Wakefield, in the same work, p. 362. In *The New SCM Dictionary of Christian Spirituality*, ed. P. Sheldrake, London, SCM Press, 2005, S. N. Schneiders, having said that 'Spirituality ... is notoriously difficult to define', goes on to say, 'Spirituality as lived experience can be defined as conscious involvement in the project of life integration through self-transcendence towards the ultimate value one perceives. This general definition is broad enough to embrace both Christian and non-Christian religious spiritualities. However, it is also specific enough to give the term some recognisable content.' (p. 1)

8 Marcion (died about AD 160) rejected the Old Testament and also certain parts of the New, for he claimed that the Christian gospel was wholly one of love. He understood the God of the Old Testament as Creator God, Demiurge, having nothing in common with the God of Jesus Christ. The early Church came to regard him as a heretic.

9 I hope to be able to return to this wider subject of the Old Testament and Christian spirituality in a further project.

10 J. G. Gammie, *Holiness in Israel*, Minneapolis, Fortress Press, 1989.

11 R. Otto, *The Idea of the Holy*, tr. J.W. Harvey, Oxford, Oxford University Press, 1923, p. 63.

12 H. Wildberger, *Isaiah 13–27* (Continental Commentary), tr. T. H. Trapp, Minneapolis, Fortress Press, 1997, p. 282.

13 See above, pp. 70-81.

14 K. Armstrong, *A History of Jerusalem: One City, Three Faiths*, London, HarperCollins, 1996, pp. xii-xiv.

15 The dating of Aristeas is disputed. For details and discussion see L. L. Grabbe, *Judaism from Cyrus to Hadrian*, London, SCM Press, 1994, pp. 179-180.

16 The Letter of Aristeas, paragraphs 83-84 as in C. T. R. Hayward, *The Jewish Temple: A non-biblical sourcebook*, London and New York, Routledge, 1996, p. 27.

17 It will be observed that I am not making any reference to the so-called 'Zion tradition', that is the notion found in some psalms (in particular Psalms 46, 48, 76) about the inviolability of Jerusalem, and that is frequently associated with the accounts of the unsuccessful attempt on the part of the Assyrian ruler Sennacherib to

defeat and enter Jerusalem in 701 BC. A. F. Kirkpatrick in his
commentary of 1902 on the Psalms considered that these psalms
originated out of that 701 BC experience, while later G. von Rad
would argue that that belief in the inviolability of Jerusalem was
shared by the prophet Isaiah and proclaimed by him (G. von Rad,
Old Testament Theology, Vol. II, Edinburgh and London, Oliver and
Boyd, 1965, pp. 155-158). I consider that the passages in Isaiah that
speak of the remarkable deliverance of the city from the Assyrian
had an earlier setting in the books of Kings and that the incorpor-
ation of them into the Isaiah book was intended to speak about
the great change in fortunes of Jerusalem, pre- and post-exile.
See above, pp. 57-62. It should be added that other Isaianic texts
which it has been argued lend weight to the so-called 'Zion tradition' are capable of being understood in different ways. Thus
Isaiah 9.4-5 ('For the yoke ... fuel for the fire') I have argued is a
generalised vision of a coming ideal Judean king under whose rule
Judah and Jerusalem will prosper (see M. E. W. Thompson,
'Isaiah's Ideal King', *JSOT* 24 (1982), pp. 79-88), while Isaiah 29.7-
8 is a generalised and generalising assurance that the purposes of
the Lord especially in regard to the chosen city of Jerusalem will
ultimately be triumphant.

18 On this chapter, see M. E. W. Thompson, 'Vision, Reality and
Worship: Isaiah 33' *ExpTim* 113 (2001-2002), pp. 327-333, where
inter alia I offer some comments on the difficulty of the presence
of ships in Jerusalem! Also, see above, pp. 52-54.

19 See, e.g., G. I. Emmerson, *Isaiah 56–66* (Old Testament Guides),
Sheffield, JSOT Press, 1992.

20 In Jeremiah there are 17 references to Zion, in Amos 2, Hosea
none, Micah 9, Obadiah 2, Zephaniah 2, and Zechariah 8.

21 So e.g. 6.11; 8.4; 9.9; chapter 10. The announcement in 40.9
is to 'the cities of Judah', yet no town is mentioned specifically.
See also 64.10. This is in some contrast to other prophetic books
in which there is more frequent mention of places other than
the main cities of Israel and Judah, Samaria and Jerusalem
respectively.

22 The expression occurs in 48.2 and 52.1.

23 So also in similar fashion four other times in chapters 40 to 55, only
twice in Psalms (146.10; 147.12) and once in Zephaniah (3.16-17).

24 See Matthew 5.14. The reference here is in all likelihood to

Jerusalem. See, e.g., E. Schweitzer, *The Good News according to Matthew*, London, SPCK, 1976, p. 99.

25 See Psalm 137.2-4; A. Curtis, *Psalms* (Epworth Commentaries), Peterborough, Epworth Press, 2004, p. 250.

26 See, e.g., Blenkinsopp, *Isaiah 40–55*, pp. 247, 311.

27 It is surely significant that the same prophet who does not speak about the restoration of sacrificial temple worship is also the one who speaks of the forgiveness of sins through those sins being laid upon a human individual, and, further, that one of the ways he employs to speak about the ministry of this individual servant, or these servants, is in the language of sacrifice. See 52.13—53.12, especially 53.10, 12; on this passage see above, pp. 76-80 and also Thompson, *Isaiah 40–66*, pp. 100-114.

28 Or however the Hebrew word here is to be translated. Compare NRSV's 'coastlands'.

29 Augustine, *City of God*, Book XIX, Chapter 16. I am indebted to Rowan Williams, *Lost Icons: Reflections on Cultural Bereavement*, London and New York, Continuum, 2003, p. 60, for this reference to Augustine.

30 T. Hunt, *Building Jerusalem: The Rise and Fall of the Victorian City*, London, Weidenfeld & Nicolson, 2004, p. 242.

31 J. H. Muirhead, *Nine Famous Birmingham Men*, Birmingham, 1909, p. 100, quoted by Hunt, (see previous note), p. 242.

32 Hunt, in the same work, p. 245, quoting W. Wilson, *The Life of George Dawson*, Birmingham, 1905, p. 152.

33 W. H. Auden, *Collected Poems*, ed. E. Mendelson, London, Faber and Faber, 1976, pp. 159-193.

34 William Blake, 'Milton'. The text quoted here is as in *William Blake: The Complete Poems*, ed. A. Ostiker, London, Penguin Books, 1977, pp. 513-634, lines 1-8. On William Blake's use of the Bible see C. Rowland, 'Blake and the Bible: Biblical Exegesis in the Work of William Blake', pp. 168-184 in J. M. Court (ed.) *Biblical Interpretation: The Meanings of Scripture – Past and Present*, London and New York, T & T Clark, 2003.

35 K. Armstrong, *A History of Jerusalem: One City, Three Faiths*, London, Harper Collins, 1996, pp. 420-421.

36 K. Armstrong, in the same work, p. 430.

SELECT BIBLIOGRAPHY

I have endeavoured to write this book with the needs of those who
might turn to the Epworth Commentary series, or similar series, for help
in their study and understanding of the Bible. Thus in what precedes
my most general reference to 'further details' on this or that passage,
issue, question is to the two volumes among the Epworth Commentaries
on the book of Isaiah. They are:

D. Stacey, *Isaiah 1–39* (Epworth Commentary), London, Epworth
    Press, 1993.
M. E. W. Thompson, *Isaiah 40–66* (Epworth Commentary),
    Peterborough, Epworth Press, 2001.

Then there are a number of commentaries on Isaiah which along with
the above two I refer to sufficiently frequently that I have given them in
short-title form. First here are the two very useful volumes in the New
Century Bible series, where Clements and Whybray between them continue to be good guides to the book.

R. E. Clements, *Isaiah 1–39* (New Century Bible), London, Marshall,
    Morgan and Scott, 1980.
R. N. Whybray, *Isaiah 40–66* (New Century Bible), London, Oliphants,
    1975.

Next there are the two volumes in the North American series of Bible
commentaries for teaching and preaching, namely,

C. R. Seitz, *Isaiah 1–39* (Interpretation: A Bible Commentary for
    Teaching and Preaching), Louisville, Kentucky, John Knox Press,
    1993.
P. D. Hanson, *Isaiah 40–66* (Interpretation: A Bible Commentary for
    Teaching and Preaching), Louisville, Kentucky, John Knox Press,
    1995.

And last but by no means least in my list of commmentaries to which I make short-title reference are the three volumes in the Anchor Bible series, a new translation with introduction and commentary, all by J. Blenkinsopp. These are all excellent, having masses of detail, but perhaps on the whole for those who do wish to 'go deeper' into the book of Isaiah.

J. Blenkinsopp, *Isaiah 1–39* (Anchor Bible), New York, Doubleday, 2000.

J. Blenkinsopp, *Isaiah 40–55* (Anchor Bible), New York, Doubleday, 2002.

J. Blenkinsopp, *Isaiah 56–66* (Anchor Bible), New York, Doubleday, 2003.

Then the commentaries of three authors who all seek to help us to understand the various parts of Isaiah in the light of the whole book, and all of them in series that are intended for general readers as well as students. These are:

J. F. A. Sawyer, *Isaiah Volume I* [chapters 1 to 32] (The Daily Study Bible), Edinburgh, St Andrew Press, 1984.

J. F. A. Sawyer, *Isaiah Volume II* [chapters 33 to 66] (The Daily Study Bible), Edinburgh, St Andrew Press, 1986.

W. Brueggemann, *Isaiah 1–39* (Westminster Bible Commentary), Louisville, Kentucky, Westminster John Knox Press, 1998.

W. Brueggemann, *Isaiah 40–66* (Westminster Bible Commentary), Louisville, Kentucky, Westminster John Knox Press, 1998.

J. Goldingay, *Isaiah* (New International Bible Commentary), Peabody, Massachusetts, Hendrickson Publishers (also Carlisle, Paternoster Press), 2001.

Now, two authors whose commentaries are written on the understanding that the whole book of Isaiah comes from one prophet:

A. Motyer, *The Prophecy of Isaiah*, Leicester, Inter-Varsity Press, 1993.

J. N. Oswalt, *The Book of Isaiah Chapters 1–39* (New International Commentary on the Old Testament), Grand Rapids, Eerdmans, 1986.

J. N. Oswalt, *The Book of Isaiah Chapters 40–66* (New International Commentary on the Old Testament), Grand Rapids, Eerdmans, 1998.

I turn to works other than commentaries about the book of Isaiah. Helpful as regards the matter of the redaction, editing of the prophetical books is,

T. Collins, *The Mantle of Elijah: The Redaction Criticism of the Prophetical Books*, Sheffield, JSOT Press, 1993.

For a useful series of essays that reflects recent trends in the study of the book of Isaiah see,

R. F. Melugin and M. A. Sweeney, ed., *New Visions of Isaiah*, JSOTSup, Sheffield, Sheffield Academic Press, 1996.

About the enormous influence that the book of Isaiah has had on the language and imagery of the Christian Church there is,

J. F. A. Sawyer, *The Fifth Gospel: Isaiah in the History of Christianity*, Cambridge, Cambridge University Press, 1996.

To help and encourage us to use Isaiah in the life of the Church today see,

C. R. Seitz, ed., *Reading and Preaching the Book of Isaiah*, Philadelphia, Fortress Press, 1988.

For those who may wish to have more detailed introduction to the book of Isaiah than is available in mine, there are the three compact and well-regarded volumes in the Sheffield Old Testament Guides series,

J. Barton, *Isaiah 1–39* (Old Testament Guides), Sheffield, Sheffield Academic Press, 1995.
R. N. Whybray, *The Second Isaiah* (Old Testament Guides), Sheffield, JSOT Press, 1983.
G. I. Emmerson, *Isaiah 56–66* (Old Testament Guides), Sheffield, Sheffield Academic Press, 1992.

Then some further books on various aspects of the Isaiah book. Mention should be made of two books about the 'servant' passages, the first something old and the second something new:

C. R. North, *The Suffering Servant in Deutero-Isaiah: An Historical and Critical Study*, Oxford, Oxford University Press, 1948, 1956.

W. H. Bellinger, Jr. and W. R. Farmer, *Jesus and the Suffering Servant:*
    Isaiah 53 and Christian Origins, Harrisburg, Pennsylvania, Trinity
    Press International, 1998.

Recently B. S. Childs has added to his books on Isaiah a study of how
in the history of the Christian Church the book of Isaiah has been inter-
preted as scripture for the Church:

B. S. Childs, *The Struggle to Understand Isaiah as Christian Scripture*,
    Grand Rapids and Cambridge, Eerdmans, 2004.

And finally, in the notes to this present work are details of various further books and commentaries on Isaiah to which reference may be
made.

ACKNOWLEDGEMENTS

Every effort has been made to fulfil the requirements with regard to reproducing copyright material. The author and publishers apologise for any possible inadvertent omissions and will be pleased to rectify them in subsequent editions of this work.

The quotations on pages 42 and 159–60 from Augustine, *City of God* are taken from St Augustine, *Concerning The City of God against the Pagans*, a new translation by Henry Bettenson, in the Penguin Classics series, London 1972, 1984, pp. 573, 593 and 876, and are reproduced by permission of Penguin Books Ltd.

The quotation on page 146 from *The Letter of Aristeas* is taken from C. T. R. Hayward, *The Jewish Temple: A non-biblical sourcebook*, London and New York, Routledge, 1996, p. 27, and is reproduced by permission of Taylor and Francis Books UK.

The three quotations on page 160 from Tristram Hunt, *Building Jerusalem: the Rise and Fall of the Victorian City*, London, Weidenfeld & Nicolson, 2004, are from pp. 242 and 245, and reproduced by permission of Weidenfeld & Nicolson, an imprint of The Orion Publishing Group.

The quotation on page 161 from W. H. Auden's 'New Year Letter' is taken from W. H. Auden, *Collected Poems*, ed. E. Mendelson, London, Faber and Faber, 1976, and reproduced by permission of the publishers Faber and Faber Ltd.

The two quotations on page 162 from Karen Armstrong, *A History of Jerusalem: One City, Three Faiths*, London, HarperCollins, 1996, are from pp. 420–21 and 430, and reproduced by permission of HarperCollins Publishers Ltd, © 1996 Karen Armstrong.

INDEX OF BIBLICAL REFERENCES

A number of passing references in this work are not included in this index. Page numbers in **bold type** indicate a principal discussion of the verse or verses concerned.

INDEX OF AUTHORS

INDEX OF NAMES AND SUBJECTS